Saint Michael the Archangel

SAINT MICHAEL THE ARCHANGEL

JAMES F. DAY

Our Sunday Visitor
Huntington, Indiana

Nihil Obstat
Msgr. Michael Heintz, Ph.D.
Censor Librorum

Imprimatur
✠ Kevin C. Rhoades
Bishop of Fort Wayne-South Bend
April 8, 2020

The *Nihil Obstat* and *Imprimatur* are official declarations that a book is free from doctrinal or moral error. It is not implied that those who have granted the *Nihil Obstat* and *Imprimatur* agree with the contents, opinions, or statements expressed.

Prayer to St. Michael for Paratroopers written by Peter S. Griffin, 101st Airborne Division, Co. A, 2/502nd PIR-DMOR, Silver Star Medal Recipient, Vietnam 1965-66 and Gold Star Brother.

26 25 24 23 3 4 5 6 7 8 9

Our Sunday Visitor Publishing Division
Our Sunday Visitor, Inc.
200 Noll Plaza
Huntington, IN 46750
1-800-348-2440
www.osv.com

ISBN: 978-1-68192-588-2 (Inventory No. T2455)

1. RELIGION—Christian Theology—History.
2. RELIGION—Christian Living—Spiritual Warfare.
3. RELIGION—Christianity—Catholic.

eISBN: 978-1-68192-589-9

LCCN: 2020936030

Cover and interior design: Chelsea Alt
Cover art: Our Sunday Visitor file art
Interior art: Paul Badde; Workman; Public domain: David Gerard, Eugène Romain Thirion, Enryonthecloud, José Rafael Aragón, Manuel Arbós y Ayerbe; Creative Commons: Livioandronico2013, KedilerNicole, Chensiyuan, Amaustan, Elio Pallard, Cesare Nebbia, Aleksei m; James Day; Susan Synek

Printed in the United States of America

Finally, be strong in the Lord and in the strength of his might. Put on the whole armor of God, that you may be able to stand against the wiles of the devil. For we are not contending against flesh and blood, but against the principalities, against the powers, against the world rulers of this present darkness, against the spiritual hosts of wickedness in the heavenly places. Therefore take the whole armor of God that you may be able to withstand in the evil day, and having done all, to stand. Stand therefore, having fastened the belt of truth around your waist, and having put on the breastplate of righteousness, and having shod your feet with the equipment of the gospel of peace; besides all these, taking the shield of faith, with which you can quench all the flaming darts of the Evil One. And take the helmet of salvation, and the sword of the Spirit, which is the word of God.

— Ephesians 6:10–17

In memory of
Father James V. Schall, SJ
1928–2019
May he rest with the angels.

Table of Contents

Foreword

I still recall with great fondness my years as an altar server at my home parish of St. Agnes in Springfield, Illinois, where the priest who trained me, Father John Sohm, was a great influence in my hearing the call of the priesthood in the Diocese of Springfield, Illinois. The way in which Father Sohm celebrated the Mass and prayed made a deep impression on me. I remember especially from those years the Prayer to Saint Michael at the end of Mass, which we as a faith community would recite together. It was a simple yet powerful exhortation to God's fearless protector, Saint Michael, that was promulgated by Pope Leo XIII, the compelling story of which you will read in the pages to come.

It is the communion of saints, but in particular Saint Michael and Our Blessed Mother, to whom the faithful have turned to in the darkest times, that they intercede to God for the mercy, peace, and grace of Our Lord Jesus Christ. This is no less true in our time as we have witnessed a dangerous increase in diabolic movements.

Following Pope Francis's summons in 2018 to recite the Saint Michael prayer, other bishops and I asked all parishes to pray for Saint Michael the Archangel's intercession at the conclusion of all Masses for the month of October, during a year that brought devastating and disheartening news that there is much still to be done to cleanse and purify the Church. Here in Orange, we said this prayer beginning September 23, the feast of Saint John of Capistrano, our secondary patron. The great prayer to the prince of the heavenly hosts was recited in English, Spanish, and Vietnamese. To this day, I am strengthened in hope that God's angels will not abandon our prayers, and I pray they faithfully carry all our petitions to our Heavenly Father.

Following the Lord's call to holiness is not an easy journey, and times of crises certainly test our resolve. I believe it is important at such a time, even if it might be difficult, to remember the words of the psalmist, "Trust in him at all times, O people; pour out your heart before him; God is a refuge for us" (Ps 62:8). Also, Saint Michael and the presence of whole choirs of angels, who we see frequently appear in pivotal parts of Scripture, remind us that spiritual warfare is indeed a reality and not to be taken lightly. It affects us all, in our own way, and we all know that life's trials are very real. Every day, indeed every moment, presents a choice for us to do well and avoid evil (see 1 Th 5:22).

The Church helps prepare the faithful in spiritual combat beginning with baptism, particularly with these questions: "Do you reject Satan? And all his works? And all his empty promises?" Many of us have heard them, and have had the chance to renew these promises at the baptisms of family members, and at the Easter Vigil as well. The light of Christ is far more attractive than any of those empty works and promises from the evil one, and I encourage all to exercise a simple examination of conscience when faced with temptation: Will this bring me closer to God? My parents, especially my father, taught us to always do the hard thing, which is the right thing, and often the "narrow door."

I remember, as a priest early on in my ministry, being witnessed to by a woman religious to "put on the whole armor of God" (Eph 6:11). Similarly, as Saint Paul also says, the word of God is our sword (see Eph 6:17). One of the most powerful and moving moments during the Sacrament of Holy Orders is the laying on of hands by the bishop to those being ordained. This significant gesture is echoed as far back as Psalms: "Blessed be the LORD, my rock, who trains my hands for war, and my fingers for battle" (Ps 144:1). Solemn moments such as these indicate both the sacramental and mystical elements of our faith. The more we are attuned to invisible movements of the sacred, the deeper our faith and prayer life will become.

There is a line attributed to Saint Ignatius of Antioch, "Wherever Jesus Christ is, there is the Catholic Church." What would follow then, in the communion of saints, is that wherever Christ is, the holy angels and saints are not too far away. Saint Michael, whose name means in Hebrew "Who is like unto God?," most certainly hovers near the glory of the Triune God. Thus, it is a great lack that we often overlook our own rich Church calendar which reflects all of these saints, who are daily gifts to help on our path to holiness and combat evil. Every day offers unique feasts and commemorations, frequently reflected in the day's Liturgy of the Hours and Mass prayers. Their purpose is to mark the hours of the day with prayer, especially calling to mind how the saints enter our lives daily. I encourage you as you read this book to foster a wholly Catholic mind, to be not afraid of expanding and deepening it, and to come to know the amazing dimensions of the Faith in an intimate way that reveals to us the presence of God.

As you will see, Saint Michael is invested in all of these dimensions, venerated first by our Jewish brothers and sisters, and celebrated in our own Church history. Time and again, Saint Michael appears when our forebears in faith needed spiritual reinforcement. The Prayer to Saint Michael, as Pope Saint John Paul II believed and as Pope Francis has reiterated in our time, helps in the battle against the forces of darkness. Learning more about the great impact of Saint Michael, as this book shows us, will help strengthen our great resolve and discipline in following Christ in response to the voice and light that calls to each of us "Come, follow me."

To this end, we can again draw strength from Saint Paul, who urges us, "Be strong in the Lord and in the strength of his might" (Eph 6:10). May God empower us also, through the intercessions of Saint Michael and Our Lady of Guadalupe as the Patroness of the Diocese of Orange, who tells us (as well as her Son), "Do not be afraid!" May all of the holy angels and saints protect us in this spiritual battle here on earth, so that we may join the Church in eternity giving praise to the Lord, in the everlasting light of his face.

✠Kevin W. Vann, Bishop of Orange
Campus of Christ Cathedral
Feast of the Archangels

Author's Note

I was introduced to the mysteries of the Catholic Faith off the shores of a great lake, past wheezing factory smokestacks, at a parish church named for a warrior angel of peace. From the outside, St. Michael's appears nondescript, just down the main street from the Methodist, Presbyterian, and Lutheran churches, as well as the dentist, barber, and bike shop. This town of seven thousands souls is a slice of midwestern Americana, exemplified by the town's name: Independence. Mystery surrounds the origin of Independence, Ohio's Catholic church. One of the oldest communities established in the Diocese of Cleveland, it was founded under the name St. Lawrence Mission Church in 1851. When a parish rather than a mission had to be created to accommodate the growing immigrant population within a generation, records showed a new name was given. Those records do not go into further specifics as to why.

The Catholic intellectual, artistic, and social traditions are commonly anchored and experienced at the parish church. For me, the sacraments of Baptism, Confession, First Communion, and Confirmation all transpired under the same crucifix, the same stained-glass windows. As I entered, breathed in the lingering aroma of incense, dipped fingertips into the holy water font, genuflected while rays of light glistened through the stained-glass windows, suddenly the Church became to my childhood imagination less a building built by post–World War II human hands and more a metaphysical ship traveling through sacred dimensions. As such, the Liturgy of the Eucharist, I now realize far better than I grasped back then, is an event far more than a meal. At Mass, we may have been physically in Independence; but every time the priest, acting *in persona Christi*, consecrated the bread and wine, there we were in fact transported: to the Last Supper and the Crucifixion, historical events and places that transcend both time and place.

In this sacred place, I joined the ranks of altar servers and later ushers, there I pondered my own vocational paths, learned devotions, attached myself to various saints, and honed the basics of faith through family examples and reading the prolific writings for children by Father Lawrence J. Lovasik, SVD. And, inevitably, this same church was my principal gateway into the reality of death, participating in funerals for family, friends and neighbors, grandparents, and my father. Here, also, my earliest memories were shaped, from the thunderous — to a child's ear — collective responses of the congregation to the sounds of wholly otherworldly organ music (and, to be fair, the music of the 1980s folk Mass).

But the church's tiny side chapel, sectioned off by two heavy doors with grills on its small windows, was where my Catholic worldview was established and nurtured. Here the Blessed Sacrament lay in quiet, dignified repose. Here adorers kept vigil in perpetual adoration, never failing to be present before the Eucharistic Lord even on pitch black, frigid winter nights.

Of all my earliest memories of St. Michael's, perhaps the most privileged were the occasions when I would accompany my mom past those metal doors and spend some quiet moments in that tiny chapel. *Who are these other silent people?* I thought, looking around. The place felt and smelled like the main church, but somehow different, like a sanctuary, a refuge, a cave.

The adoration chapel reminded me of another mysterious place: the crypt at the Cathedral of Saint John the Evangelist, the final resting place for the deceased bishops of the diocese. Yet this chapel was not a crypt, but a wellspring for a Catholic life, a place to set forth one's fears and trials, to acknowledge flaws and faults, to think about the demands and graces of that life in total silence, save for the occasional turning of a page or creaking of a kneeler. Indeed, though the chapel was silent, it was at times possible to hear the infrequent passing siren from an ambulance or fire truck, the rumble of machinery, or the honk of an irritated car horn from the world outside. Such were occasions for prayer, and here, in this place, was refuge from chaos.

My young eyes often drifted to the small, square, stained-glass window depicting a terrifying image. Terrifying, if one focused only on the writhing, angry demon pinned down by the sure foot of an angel. Around these two figures was a dark, desolate, rocky landscape, surrounded by pockets of flames. Terrifying, yet stirring, if I contemplated the hero in the image: the armor-clad angel, cloaked in a flowing gold cape, wings extended, scales in his left hand, his right hand clutching a long-sword. He was the personification of victory, righteousness, and justice.

"Who is that, Mom?" I once asked, gazing at the angel, when I could finally articulate what had long steeped in my childhood consciousness.

"That's who our church is named after," my mother replied quietly. "That's Saint Michael."

This book tells that archangel's story, he who dutifully served the Face of God from before time as we know it began, and won the love of Jew and Gentile alike during Israel's history and the spread of Christendom. Whoever discovers him will meet a most powerful intercessor, one who leaves his angelic footprint wherever he appears and on the souls who encounter him. Even in Independence, Ohio.

Introduction

The Role of Saint Michael in Today's Crisis

There is little doubt that the crisis in the Catholic Church today is both enormous and disturbing. The enduring sex abuse scandal is mind-numbing. Scores of Catholics have left the Faith altogether. Division, unrest, violence, and mistreatment of others seem acceptable ways of life. The dictatorship of relativism commands that there is no one objective and absolute truth. The ensuing free-for-all has revealed the depravity and hollowness of our supposed enlightened society.

What Pope Francis calls the "globalization of indifference" causes many of us to shrug when we observe such a landscape. For the indifferent, this is how the world is — as it always was, and likely will always be. But from the Catholic perspective, in past eras, saints and martyrs have arisen out of similar turmoil to reshape the world and the Faith. The only answer strong enough to combat centuries of scandal and turmoil is Jesus Christ. It is only in our pride that we think such an answer is weak and ineffective.

Today there are souls who, in the name of Christ, will rise above the heinous scandals of sex abuse and moral corruption, unbelief and ridicule, to renew the Faith. Even in her darkest hours, the Church never fails to manifest the Eucharistic Lord at every Mass on every day throughout the world. The Church has a trove of inspiration to fortify her faithful through each day's struggles. Christ also sends His Blessed Mother and the saints to remind us we are not alone. He also sends His angels, ready and willing to do His will. There is one angel in particular primed for crises and battles: we know him as Saint Michael.

Saint Michael remains a popular subject of study, devotion, shrines, monasteries, invocations of prayers, and inspiration to overcome spiritual struggles. As this work will show, he consistently emerges in dire times when the faithful are desperate for protection and guidance. How has such interest in Saint Michael the Archangel remained so strong? On the one hand, so esteemed was Michael in Jewish tradition that he earned the title Protector of Israel. In turn, his exalted role as protector and defender of the Catholic Church and Vatican City, which has earned him titles such as Guardian of Purgatory, Guardian of the Blessed Sacrament, and Guardian of the Pope, offers a strong case for continuity between Judaism and Christianity. This ecumenical nature of Michael has continued beyond Judeo-Christian traditions. Even those without any particular religious affiliation, yet interested in angelology, view and respect Michael and the archangels as powerful numinous beings capable of influencing our lives here on earth.

On the other hand, the presence of evil has not abated in our own time. Quite the opposite: Satan and his minions appear to be as destructive as ever. The reputation of the Church as the world's moral authority has practically evaporated. What was once a beacon of hope guiding souls toward the eternal peace of Christ is now regarded with suspicion and mistrust. One cannot help but be tempted to wonder if evil has indeed infiltrated and corrupted good; if evil may have the last say after all.

Pope Pius XII (1939–1958) continually expressed his concern at the erosion of facing life from a wholly Catholic worldview. As early as 1946, he detected a prevalent loss of the sense of sin. In his 1950 encyclical *Humani Generis*, Pope Pius directly confronted the various ways in which he believed the Faith was becoming undermined. Among these was gradually increasing doubt in the supernatural and those who occupy it. The pope noted, "Some question whether angels are personal beings, and whether matter and spirit differ essentially. Others destroy the gratuity of the supernatural order. ... Some pervert the very concept of original sin. ... Some even say that the doctrine of transubstantiation ... should be so modified that the real presence of Christ in the Holy Eucharist be reduced to a kind of symbolism."

The pontiff's concerns foreshadowed the creeping relativism of later decades. His list above from 1950 unfortunately remains relevant today. The second half of the twentieth century showed a replacement of the responsibilities of true liberty and freedom with libertinism — a hedonistic viewpoint with disastrous results in the breakdown of family life, widespread use of pornography, technological isolation, loss of sense of community, and mental and physical health issues.

In *The Art of War*, Sun Tzu advises: "If you know the enemy and know yourself, you need not fear the result of a hundred battles. If you know yourself but not the enemy, for every victory gained you will also suffer a defeat. If you know neither the enemy nor yourself, you will succumb in every battle." The War in Heaven that established Saint Michael as defender of all those seeking the good, true, and beautiful was not just a battle like those that have transpired between warring nations over the centuries. Though that victory was secured by the good angels, it does not mean the known enemy, Satan, has retired from the war. Nor does it mean that human souls are spared from combat. Every soul is a battlefield.

Saint Michael continues to wage war on our behalf, wading into the dark recesses of sin, suffering, struggle, and despair. He leads his armies where others fear to tread. We have only been obscured by our limited vision into thinking he and his fellow angels are not there.

An afflicted time as ours, as we yearn for signs of hope, is precisely the right moment for renewed communication with the invisible, including Michael and the angels. It is precisely now when his great, fearless, selfless gifts are most needed.

Attacks from Within

On June 29, 1972, Pope Saint Paul VI declared in a homily on the feast of Saints Peter and Paul, "Through some crack, the smoke of Satan has entered the temple of God." The turbulence of modernity and the confusion in the wake of the Second Vatican Council stymied Paul VI. To use the United States as an example, in 1965, there were 58,632 priests in the country. In 2018, the number was 36,580, even as the number of registered Catholics grew.[1] Religious sisters tallied 45,605 in 2018, compared to 179,954 in 1965. As Bishop Robert Barron remarked in a presentation to the United States Conference of Catholic Bishops in the summer of 2019, "50% of millennial Catholics now claim no religious identity." The vast majority of those who consider themselves fallen away Catholics are so great as to constitute their own religion. "The reduction in the number of faithful will lead to [the Church] losing an important part of its social privileges," then-Father Joseph Ratzinger foresaw in 1970. "It will become small and will have to start pretty much all over again."

In an April 1994 *Regina Coeli* address in Saint Peter's Square, Pope John Paul II reminded the faithful about the reality of spiritual combat. Referencing Ephesians 6:10 — "Finally, be strong in the Lord and in the strength of his might" — the pope stated, "It is the same battle the Book of the Apocalypse (Revelation) refers to, recalling before our eyes the image of Saint Michael the Archangel."

The pontiff urged the faithful to recommit themselves to praying Leo XIII's Prayer of Saint Michael.

Tragically, the clerical sexual abuse scandal and related scandals of malfeasance and mismanagement surfaced in the same era John Paul so inspiringly called a "new springtime of the human spirit" in his speech to the United Nations in October 1995. On the one hand, while the crimes and cover-ups decimated Church credibility, we can see in the catastrophe the widespread demonic infiltration that Paul VI had sensed in 1972.

Pointing out the Great Accuser's lies and deceptions has also been a priority for Pope Francis. The blessing of the Saint Michael statue in the Vatican Gardens in July 2013 was attended by both Pope Francis and Pope Emeritus Benedict XVI. Pope Francis spoke to those gathered, and after acknowledging that this monument to Saint Michael had begun under Benedict's pontificate, added:

> This sculpture reminds us therefore that evil is vanquished, the accuser is unmasked, his head is crushed, because salvation was fulfilled once and for all by the blood of Christ. Even if the devil is always trying to scratch the face of the Archangel and the face of man, God is stronger; his is the victory and his salvation is offered to every human being. On the journey and in the trials of life we are not alone, we are accompanied and sustained by the Angels of God, who offer, so to speak, their wings to help us overcome the many dangers, to be able to fly above those realities that can make our lives difficult or drag us down. In consecrating the Vatican City State to Saint Michael the Archangel, let us ask him to defend us from the Evil One and cast him out.

Across the Tiber from Saint Peter's looms the giant statue of St. Michael above the parapet of the imposing, ancient Castel Sant'Angelo, preparing to sheathe his sword in victory, a striking visual that has endured for centuries emphasizing Saint Michael's role in our mortal lives and immortal souls. Still, with such spiritual protection over Rome, how has such moral depravity and corruption wrought by some members of the Mystical Body of Christ, which has caused such devastation for victims and the Church itself, been allowed to happen?

Blessed Anne Catherine Emmerich's Vision

Blessed Anne Catherine Emmerich (1774–1824) was a German mystic and stigmatic revered by many for her powerfully realistic visions, most notably published in *The Dolorous Passion of Our Lord Jesus Christ* and *The Life of the Blessed Virgin Mary*. She was also an Augustinian nun and frequently appears in images as bedridden, wearing a bandage around her head and clutching a crucifix. "She showed us the value of sacrifice and compassion for the Crucified Lord," John Paul II professed in a 1987 visit to Germany. Of her prolific visions, the mystic detailed a specific one from September 29, 1820, Michaelmas Day, that involved Saint Michael.[2]

The vision describes with stunning imagery many of the places, events, and people we will meet in this book. Michael takes her soaring past Mont-Saint-Michel, the landmark site detailed in chapter 5; she sees how much of Catholic France venerated him as patron before glimpsing Monte Gargano in Italy, another major shrine covered in chapter 5; she observes a purgatorial image of souls repenting their sins; Michael then shows her the noble work of the guardian angels, as well as the destructive work of the fallen angels. In an especially innovative touch, the vision shows the guardian angels as tireless, fervent, committed to peace for the whole of mankind, while pleasing God above all else. The bad angels, however, are shown to embody the deadly sins by languishing and lounging about, given over to laziness and indifference. Their demeanors are irascible, unpleasant; they constantly bark at each other. Blessed Anne Catherine Emmerich sees how easily these loathsome creatures transfer these vices to humans, successfully leading mankind away from God and their heaven-oriented purpose.

The vision continues. After preserving the sanctity of a church dedicated to him in Rome, Michael takes Anne Catherine to the Himalayas, where she witnesses a purgatory-like state where souls pay off their sins by working strenuously at a mill amid a climate of ice and snow. Finally, Blessed Anne Catherine Emmerich finds herself in the heavenly realm, and there glimpses Michael harmoniously accompanied by the other archangels. Here she describes Michael's appearance: "Michael wore a helmet with a crest of rays, and his body seemed encased in armor and girt with cords, his robe descending to the knees like a fringed apron. In one hand he held a long staff surmounted by a cross under which floated the standard of the Lamb; in the other was a flaming sword. His feet also were laced."

Blessed Anne then details seeing the glory of the Trinity, the Blessed Sacrament, a tabernacle in repose, and the descent of the new Jerusalem onto the old. That vision complete, Anne is given another one, a dark view of a battle in an unknown time, which she believed occurs not far from Rome. This particular vision perhaps can be seen as an allegory for the ongoing battle forces of good must wage against the indifference and loathing of the bad angels: "I had a picture of an immense battle. The whole plain was a mass of dense smoke, and the bushes were full of soldiers who kept up an incessant fire. The place lay low, and there were great cities in the distance. When all seemed lost, Saint Michael at the invocation of one of the leaders, swept down with a legion of angels and the victory was instantly gained."

Anne also indicates a similar vision, dated December 30, with Saint Michael standing atop the cupola of Saint Peter's Basilica in Rome, where "a desperate struggle was going on below." Again, armed with his fiery sword, Michael swoops into the fray, while a "number of saints hovered in the air over the combatants." Whatever the interpretation of these private revelations, assaults on Christ and his Church are hardly new. Yet we are living in times in which the evil one's minions are running rampant, preying on the innocent, subverting God's goodness, turning gardens and vineyards into wastelands. The battle imagery described by Blessed Anne Catherine Emmerich is a metaphor for our own ongoing struggle, reminding us that the devil very much exists.

In a 2013 homily at a Mass celebrated for the Gendarmerie Corps (the police force of Vatican City), Pope Francis explained that the war between the angels of God and Satan is a war that "has been waged every day, every day: it is waged in the heart of men and women … It is the war between good and evil." Later, he encouraged Gendarmerie Corps to: "Pray often so that, with the intercession of Saint Michael the Archangel, the Lord may safeguard you from giving in to every temptation, from every temptation to corruption for money, for riches, from vanity and arrogance."

When another round of clergy-related sex scandals stormed into public light in summer 2018, headlined by actions of ex-priest, former cardinal and archbishop of Washington, Theodore E. McCarrick, as well as a damning Pennsylvania Grand Jury report that detailed years of diocesan malfeasance, morale dipped to a new low. The flood of bad news, disgust over incomprehensible actions, and sorrow for victims did not equate with the joy of the Gospel we faithful are called to proclaim.

Enter Saint Michael the Archangel.

For the month of October in 2018, Pope Francis requested both daily rosaries and the recitation of the Saint Michael Prayer, "to ward off the attacks of the devil who seeks to divide the Church."[3] Many bishops throughout the United States also issued their own directive throughout their diocese to resume the Saint Michael Prayer after Mass.

Spiritual pride can wreak irreversible havoc. Satan, even if defeated in the end, desperately seeks the ruination of souls. Near occasions of sin and the effects of sin are still prominent, unchecked, even encouraged by our culture.

We cannot go alone. We need spiritual help in putting on our armor of God.

We need Saint Michael.

1

Who Are the Angels?

Saint Paul, no stranger to the intimate relationship between the physical and spiritual, reminds us that our presence on earth is neither a mere coincidence nor a random happenstance of colliding matter: "Blessed be the God and Father of our Lord Jesus Christ, who has blessed us in Christ with every spiritual blessing in the heavenly places, even as he chose us in him before the foundation of the world, that we should be holy and blameless before him" (Eph 1:3–4). This directly challenges the belief today that nothing exists beyond the physical. Yet even amid our modern emphasis on physical experience, angels remain popular in our culture as fascinating mystical creatures. Angelology is still a subject of enduring interest across age groups, cultures, and religions. How are we to understand the movements of the supernatural?

The Archangels Michael, Gabriel & Raphael Displaying the Holy Face with Mary and St. John / Paul Badde

The Most Excellent of All Creatures

The *Catechism of the Catholic Church* is unambiguous in its description of angels as a point of faith: "The existence of the spiritual, non-corporeal beings that Sacred Scripture usually calls 'angels' is a truth of faith."[1] It is perhaps most efficient to continue using the *Catechism*'s succinct explanation of angelology:

> St. Augustine says: "'Angel' is the name of their office, not of their nature. If you seek the name of their nature, it is 'spirit'; if you seek the name of their office, it is 'angel': from what they are, 'spirit', from what they do, 'angel.'" With their whole beings the angels are *servants* and messengers of God. Because they "always behold the face of my father in heaven' they are the 'mighty ones who do his word, hearkening to the voice of his word."

As purely *spiritual* creatures angels have intelligence and will: they are personal and immortal creatures, surpassing in perfection all visible creatures, as the splendor of their glory bears witness.

Christ is the center of the angelic world. They are *his* angels. "When the Son of man comes in his glory, and all the angels with him.." They belong to him because they were created *through* and *for* him: "for in him all things were created in heaven and on earth, visible and invisible, whether thrones or dominions or principalities or authorities — all things were created through him and for him." They belong to him still more because he has made them messengers of his saving plan: "Are they not all ministering spirits sent forth to serve, for the sake of those who are to obtain salvation?" (CCC 329–331).

> We, Christ's brothers in adoption, also receive "the mysterious and powerful help of angels" (CCC 334): … From its beginning until death, human life is surrounded by their watchful care and intercession. "Beside each believer stands an angel as protector and shepherd leading him to life." (CCC 336)

The nature and mission of these beings, from the moment of their creation by God, was and remains adoration of their very Creator. Their primary goal, of fostering repentance and conversion, is summarized by Jesus in the Gospel of Luke: "I tell you, there is joy before the angels of God over one sinner who repents" (Lk 15:10).

The abundant presence of angels throughout Scripture in both the Old and New Testament reveals many aspects of their nature:

- Their role as messengers, such as St. Gabriel the Archangel's interaction with Mary of Nazareth at the Annunciation (see Lk 1:26–38) and with Zecharias announcing to him his wife will bear a son, John (Lk 1:11–20);
- Their ability to don human form in order to guard and protect, such as Raphael in the Book of Tobit (Tb 5:4ff) or the Angel and Habbakuk in the Book of Daniel (Dn 14:33–39);

- Their abundant appearances in the life of Jesus, from announcing his birth to the shepherds (Lk 2:8–15) to frequently administering to Him throughout his time on earth, including the Passion (Lk 22:43), at the empty tomb (Mt 28: 2–7), and ultimately appearing at his Ascension (Ac 1:10–11).

In his well-regarded book *The Angels*, Pascal P. Parente (1887–1971), a Catholic theologian and professor at Catholic University of America, describes the various ways angels communicate, sometimes through the spoken word of human language, but also amongst themselves. He terms the language of angels as *illumination.* This illumination reflects the depictions we see of joyous angels as rejoicing, blissful choirs. The sixth-century theologian Pseudo-Dionysius (not to be confused with Dionysius the Areopagite from Acts 17:34), who influenced later theologians such as St. Thomas Aquinas, writes in *De Coelesti Hierarchia* (The Celestial Hierarchy), "In perpetual purity they encompass his eternal Knowledge in that most high and eternal angelic dance, rapt in the bliss of manifold blessed contemplations, and irradiated with pure and primal splendors."

Question 53 of the Prima Pars of the *Summa Theologiae* deals directly with the movement of angels. How can spiritual beings without physical bodies permeate time and space? Saint Thomas likens the capability of angels to transcend such physical limitations by citing that it was Christ's soul which descended into Hell, while his body lay in repose in the tomb of Joseph of Arimathea in Jerusalem. "Therefore," Saint Thomas posits, "a beatified angel is moved locally." This does not mean angels are capable of bilocation, the miracle of appearing in two places at once, another matter Saint Thomas addressed: "Since the angel's power is finite, it does not extend to all things, but to one determined thing." This expands our horizon of understanding: angels have free will; angels can only be in one place at one time; yet within these limitations they are capable of appearing in an illusory body form, speaking and interacting with humans, communicating with each other, but not performing miracles on their own initiative. Saint Thomas says: "[A miracle] is something done by God outside the order of all created nature." Miracles can be done by God through the ministry of the angels, just as we see miracles in the lives of the saints.

The Order of Angels

Pseudo-Dionysius charted the traditionally held nine choirs (ranks) of angels as follows:

The Supreme Hierarchy

1. Seraphim (Is 6:2)
2. Cherubim (Gn 3:24)
3. Thrones (Col 1:16)

The Middle Hierarchy

1. Dominions (Col 1:16)
2. Virtues or Authorities (1 Pt 3:22; Col 1:16)
3. Powers (1 Pt 3:22)

The Lower Hierarchy

1. Principalities (Col 1:16)
2. Archangels (1 Thes 4:16)
3. Angels (1 Pt 3:22)

It has never been firmly determined how many angels were created by God at the time of their formation. "Then I looked, and I heard around the throne and the living creatures and the elders the voice of many angels, numbering myriads of myriads and thousands of thousands," the author of Revelation states (5:11). This echoes a similar statement in the book of Daniel: "A stream of fire issued and came forth from before him; a thousand thousands served him, and ten thousand times ten thousand stood before him" (7:10).

However, of all these celestial creatures, only three angels are mentioned by name in Sacred Scripture. These three are part of the same choir, but from the second lowest branch in the hierarchy of angels: that of Archangels.[2] Indeed, contrary to popular thought, archangels are viewed as only one notch above the choir of Angels, a far cry from the heightened status of Seraphim and Cherubim. And yet, because three archangels are singled out by name in scripture, they have been venerated throughout history, and their angelic holiness merited the title of "Saint." Their names are quite familiar to us: Saint Gabriel, Saint Raphael, and Saint Michael.

2
WHO IS LIKE GOD?

In order to understand Michael's place in salvation history, we must also understand Lucifer's. It might be easy to assume that Michael was always hailed as Prince of the Heavenly Hosts. As we have seen, however, Michael seems to have served in relative obscurity within the eighth choir of angels, the archangels, as we read in the epistle of Saint Jude: "But when the archangel Michael, contending with the devil, disputed about the body of Moses, he did not presume to pronounce a reviling judgment upon him, but said, 'The Lord rebuke you'" (Jude 1:9). Michael's exhortation here is later echoed in Pope Leo XIII's prayer of Saint Michael, which we will explore in chapter 7: "May God rebuke him [Satan], we humbly pray."

Still, Michael's duty to God was dictated by loyalty and humility, two traits discarded by Lucifer — so much so that Lucifer fomented open rebellion within the angelic ranks. After this act of rebellion by Lucifer, Michael's love for the Supreme Good permitted him to lead by example, through loyalty and humility, and to put his faith in action.

Jesus himself paints a visceral image of the climactic moment of the war in heaven, when his seventy-two disciples returned to report on their evangelization mission: "'Lord, even the demons are subject to us in your name!' And he said to them, 'I saw Satan fall like lightning from heaven'" (Lk 10:17–18). Here, Christ is echoing the prophet Isaiah: "How you are fallen from heaven, O Day Star, son of the Dawn!" (Is 14:12).

Tradition holds that Saint Michael himself forever cast Satan from the eternal gates. The theme of Michael as God's defender later became widely popular in the development of cults and devotions to Saint Michael throughout Christendom. Pope Saint Pius V (1566–1572), for instance, who led the Church and Holy League in the Battle of Lepanto (1571), took the name Michele upon entering the Dominican order, and frequently invoked Saint Michael during periods of darkness for the Church, particularly in the wake of the Reformation.[1]

But what would even compel a powerful angel, given such a privileged position to behold God face to face, to reject and rebel against that same Beatific Vision? It is a question that has long engrossed humanity. Saint Ambrose clarifies that while it may have been the good angels who defeated the bad, it was the choice of the bad angels to rebel and disobey that truly caused their downfall.[2] The seven deadly sins, and one in particular, motivated Lucifer and continue to motivate those who seek to destroy truth, beauty, and goodness. "Pride goes before destruction, and a haughty spirit before a fall," warns the Book of Proverbs (16:18). Of the deadly sins, pride perhaps instigates all others: anger, gluttony, greed, envy, lust, sloth, and vanity. Pride divided the angelic harmony; later, pride would lead to the fall of mankind in the sin of Adam and Eve. Satan, "the father of lies," is at the heart of both rebellions.

NON SERVIAM

"For long ago you broke your yoke and burst your bonds; and you said, 'I will not serve'" (Jer 2:20). Why and how did pride compel Lucifer to reject and rebel against the Beatific Vision, the Creator of all things, Love itself? Remember that angels are not divine but created — free will is part of their nature. Yet while Lucifer's rebellion is infamous, the reasons for it are less understood.

Revelation 12 speaks of a dragon whose "tail swept down a third of the stars of heaven, and cast them to the earth," symbolizing the third of the angels that Lucifer, henceforth known as the Devil and Satan, corrupted in his refusal to serve — to love — God (cf. Rv 12:3–4). Revelation 12 details Michael leading the good angels against this rebellion: "Now war arose in heaven, Michael and his angels fighting against the dragon; and the dragon and his angels fought, but they were defeated and there was no longer any place for them in heaven. And the great dragon was thrown down, that ancient serpent, who is called the Devil and Satan, the deceiver of the whole world—he was thrown down to the earth, and his angels were thrown down with him" (Rv 12:7–9). Michael's heroics in this war cemented his role as intercessor, protector, and guide for both nations and individuals.

Indeed, Saint John Henry Newman (1801–1890) speculated that Saint Michael was particularly present at the birth of Christ in Bethlehem on that first Christmas. Cardinal Newman also saw Michael's presence in safeguarding mother and child in King Herod's intent to kill the Messiah. This great English theologian drew this notion from the Book of Revelation, just before detailing the battle between Michael and the dragon: "Now war arose in heaven, Michael and his angels fighting against the dragon; and the dragon and his angels fought, but they were defeated and there was no longer any place for them in heaven. And the great dragon was thrown down, that ancient serpent, who is called the Devil and Satan, the deceiver of the whole world — he was thrown down to the earth, and his angels were thrown down with him" (Rv 12:1–3).

Michael, *Mi-ka-el* in Hebrew, means "Who is like God?" (in Latin, *Quis ut Deus?*) It is a question, not an answer — the One who is like God, because he is God, is Jesus Christ. Enraged and clouded by pride and envy, the one who sought to be like God could not bow before God himself. And yet, by his own free will, Satan is something like a god ... in the miserable existence that is Hell.

We often perceive Lucifer's rebellion and the ensuing war as something distant and ethereal, independent of our own interests and needs; yet that war continues to rage today. Lucifer, not content with dragging some angels to the netherworld, seeks to bring every human soul down to the pit as well.

Michael, Guardian of Israel

The Book of Daniel in the Old Testament is an essential text to understand Michael's mission throughout salvation history. Partway through the book, Daniel is in mourning after experiencing a revelation of a coming great war. Languishing on the bank of the Tigris River, Daniel is visited by an angelic presence, understood to be the archangel Gabriel, who visited Daniel previously in 9:21. Gabriel assures Daniel his prayer was heard seeking to acquire knowledge of God and to humble himself before Him. "I have come because of your words. The prince of the kingdom of Persia withstood me twenty-one days; but Michael, one of the chief princes came to help me" (10:12–13). Gabriel speaks to Daniel of Michael's role as Guardian of Israel continuing until the end of time:

> At that time shall arise Michael, the great prince who has charge of your people. And there shall be a time of trouble, such as has never been since there was a nation till that time; but at that time your people shall be delivered, every one whose name shall be found written in the book. And many of those who sleep in the dust of the earth shall awake, some to everlasting life, and some to shame and everlasting contempt. And those who are wise shall shine like the brightness of the firmament; and those who turn many to righteousness, like the stars for ever and ever. (12:1–3)

Detail of Archangel Michael on stained-glass window in St. Stephen the Martyr Daily Mass Chapel in Omaha / Workman, own work

Michael is also a prominent feature in Jewish apocrypha. While these works are not considered authoritative texts and are outside Christian tradition, they nevertheless illustrate Jewish piety, supplementing the veneration of Michael as Guardian of Israel.

One of these is *The Life of Adam and Eve*, known as *The Apocalypse of Moses* in its Greek version. Even after the banishment of Adam and Eve from Eden, these texts suggest, Michael remains present to them. In a touching scene, for example, it is Michael who assists Eve in birthing her first born, Cain: "Michael was standing to her right and touched his face to her chest and said to Eve: 'Blessed are you, Eve, on account of Adam, for his prayers and supplications are great. I was sent to you that you might receive our help. Arise now and prepare yourself for birth.'"[3] Later, by order of God, it is Michael who instructs Adam on how to farm: "The Lord God sent various seeds by Michael the angel, who gave them to Adam and showed them how to work and tend the ground, in order to have fruit, from which they and all their generations might live."[4]

In a visually striking sequence, Adam recounts for his son, Seth, his expulsion from the garden: "After I worshipped the Lord God, straightway Michael, the archangel of God, took my hand and threw me out of the paradise of God's visitation and commanding. Michael, holding in his hand a rod, touched the waters which surrounded paradise and they froze. Then I crossed over, and Michael crossed over with me and brought me again to the place from which he had taken me."[5]

Other Jewish works speak also of Michael's missions serving the Chosen People. One of these is the apocalyptic work *The Book of Enoch*, named after Enoch, the great-grandfather of Noah. Additionally, the Midrash Rabbah records Rabbi Eliezer Ben Jacob's belief that "Michael descended and rescued Abraham from the fiery furnace."[6]

And *The Testament of Abraham* is yet another text that details Michael leading a host of angels to safeguard Abraham's soul:

> And immediately the archangel Michael came with a multitude of angels and took up his precious soul in his hands in a divinely woven linen cloth, and they tended the body of the just Abraham with divine ointments and perfumes until the third day after his death, and buried him in the land of promise, the oak of Mamre, but the angels received his precious soul, and ascended into heaven, singing the hymn of "thrice holy" to the Lord the God of all, and they set it there to worship the God and Father.[7]

In these examples we see shades of what will follow in the Christian tradition: Michael does not limit his intervention to Israel alone, but continues his mission of safeguarding and protecting the pilgrim church on earth.

Castel Sant'Angelo / Livioandronico2013 / CC BY-SA (https://creativecommons.org/licenses/by-sa/4.0)

3

The Rise of Devotion to Saint Michael

So far, we have learned the archangel's primary functions in the life of faith:

1. To do battle against Satan and his minions.
2. To defend the faithful from Satan's temptations and clutches, including at death.
3. To be the chief protector of the people of God.

But how did devotion to Saint Michael expand throughout the early Christian communities so rapidly and ardently?

In Near East traditions, Saint Michael has been often called the Archistrategos, inspired by the theology of Origen of Alexandria

(A.D. 185–254). Here Michael was less a warrior angel, wielding a sword and clad in armor, than he was a healer of the sick.[1] Two stories help illustrate this title, representing both physical healing and healing of stress caused by worldly demands.

In Colossae, in modern-day Turkey, home to the Colossians, the apostles Philip and Bartholomew preached and prophesied that on a coming day Michael the Archangel would appear and miraculous deeds would follow. Indeed, on the spot the apostles predicted, a spring burst forth one day. Remarkable healings occurred for both believers and nonbelievers. Many converted to Christianity because of the spring. In nearby Laodicia, a Greek man, a non-Christian, was visited by Saint Michael and instructed to take his mute daughter to the spring. The man did so, and the girl was cured of her muteness. In thanksgiving, not only did the father oversee a church built atop the spring dedicated to Michael, but the whole family converted to Christianity. Later, in the time of Archippus, first bishop of Laodicia, enemies of the spring's miraculous powers sought to flood the area around the church and destroy it. It is believed Michael himself protected the sanctuary by diverting the rushing waters. The intervention, known as the Miracle of the Archangel Michael at Chonae, is commemorated in the Orthodox Church on September 19.

Second, in the Balkan mountain range of Osogovo, situated on a volcanic crater, is Lesnovo Monastery, also known by its official name from the fourteenth century — the Monastery of Saint Archangel Michael and Saint Hermit Gabriel of Lesnovo. A local hermit living in the eleventh century, Gabriel of Lesnovo, received a revelation from Michael to establish this monastery. In time, it became a thriving spiritual center of prayer, artistic productions, and literary creations.

But long before Christianity spread into far-flung mountain ranges, the early centuries of the Church in Jerusalem, Antioch, and Rome were a perilous and uncertain time for devoted believers. Wracked by persecutions, comprised of secret underground gatherings, it was a time of fearless martyrs and, ultimately, the fervent spread of an exciting new faith that enabled such spiritual warriors like desert hermits to reach profound spiritual heights.

It was a period of endurance for the Faith, one where Michael gained a beloved reputation as a figure who embodies what was known by the ancient Israelites: the protection of the people of God. Let's take a look at how that reputation developed.

Michael and Constantine the Great

Among those who encountered Michael's pious and unchangeable will was, of all people, the most powerful person in the entire vast Roman empire: its pagan emperor Constantine (A.D. 272–337). In early A.D. 303, the Roman emperors — Diocletian, Maximian, Galerius, and Constantine's father, Constantius — sought to crack down on the pesky Christian population, with the ruthless intention to stamp it out forever. Under Diocletian, the empire burned sacred texts, demolished churches, and tortured Christians. Yet, incredibly, emperor Galerius on his deathbed discontinued the persecutions with the Edict of Toleration in 311. At the center now was Constantine. Constantine was intent to return Rome to its imperial glory of old: one emperor, a god among men.

But this was a new era, Constantine was to discover. He learned this in a spectacular way when he experienced a vision on the eve of battle: "[Constantine] said that about noon, when the day was already beginning to decline, he saw with his own eyes the trophy of a cross of light in the heavens, above the sun, and bearing the inscription *In Hoc Signo Vinces*, 'by this sign you will conquer.' At this sight he himself was struck with amazement, and his whole army also, which followed him on this expedition, and witnessed the miracle."[2] Christ himself then instructed Constantine to use that sign in battle. Such was the development of the *labarum*, a familiar imagery in Christian art of a battle standard depicting the Chi-Rho symbol.

But just how genuine was Christian influence on Constantine? Constantine's mother, Helena, was so deeply affected by the Christian faith that she converted. She is venerated in the Church as Saint Helena, and is credited with bringing relics from the Holy Land to be housed in the reliquary of the imperial treasury of Constantinople, capital city of the Roman Empire from A.D. 330 onward. Formerly known as Byzantium and today Istanbul, Constantine identified this location in the Bosphorus strait where east meets west as a "new Rome." At its height, it was one of the world's greatest marvels, and the relics from the Holy Land, particularly the Passion relics, remained Constantinople's most sacred possessions.

Near Constantinople, the great emperor finally encountered the great archangel. Sixth-century Byzantine chronicler John Malalas details that Constantine visited a pagan temple attributed to the legendary Argonauts. According to Greek myth as related by Malalas, the Argonauts were attempting access to the Black Sea and were chased by Amykus, son of Poseidon and Melia. The Argonauts were granted a vision of an ethereal creature with wings with promise of victory. The Argonauts paid homage to this vision by constructing a shrine, which they named Sosthenios.[3] The story of its founding and the shrine itself, located about twenty kilometers north of Constantinople, intrigued Constantine. The emperor and his forces camped at the shrine. There Constantine encountered a vision that the Sosthenios shrine was to be transformed in honor of Saint Michael.[4] And so was established Michaelion, a highly popular pilgrimage site with healings and miracles attributed to Michael's intercession. An early Church historian named Sozomen personally witnessed the healings that occurred at the sanctuary: "It is believed that Michael, the Divine archangel, once appeared there. And I also affirm that this is true, because I myself received the greatest benefits." Today, Michaelion is known as the Church of the Great Archangels. Devotion to Michael rapidly spread, with up to fifteen churches dedicated to Saint Michael in the metropolis of Constantinople alone.[5]

Constantine died on May 22, 337, in Nicomedia, and was baptized purportedly on his deathbed by Eusebius. The Orthodox

Church in America refers to Constantine as "Equal of the Apostles," and while not technically a canonized saint, he is recognized in the Roman Church as a major figure in Christian history. Archbishop Piero Marini recently summarized the magnitude of Constantine's influence: "The peace of the Church at the time of Constantine had decisive consequences. As the number of baptized Christians increased, exterior signs of Christian devotion multiplied, the cult of the martyrs grew, people began to make pilgrimages, and everywhere new churches and basilicas were built."[6]

As Archbishop Marini noted, with Christianity now free to emerge from hiding in the catacombs, great churches and sanctuaries gradually arose. The influence of Saint Michael was not limited to Constantinople alone.

Michael at Gargano

Thirty kilometers north of the Italian coastal city of Manfredonia on the Adriatic Sea, about 350 kilometers from Rome, near San Giovanni Rotondo, now known as the burial site of Padre Pio, sits a sanctuary atop a mountain — the Sanctuary of Monte Sant'Angelo sul Gargano. This particular shrine laid the foundation for devotion to Michael in the West. The remarkable origin story of this sanctuary was compiled by an anonymous author in the ninth century.[7]

It is the beginning of the last decade of the fifth century. Laurence of Siponto is the local bishop. A wealthy farmer of the region, Garganus, has lost one of his bulls and is combing the slopes of his lands for the animal. To his utter surprise, he finally finds the bull kneeling at a grotto on the mountaintop. Unable to coax the beast away from his prayer-like posture, the land baron aims his bow and arrow at the bull. Yet somehow, when he releases the arrow, in a sudden gust of wind the arrow completely changes course, striking Garganus himself.

The bizarre scenario perplexed all who heard it, including Bishop Laurence. To discern the truth of Garganus's claim, Bishop Laurence practiced three days of prayer and fasting. On May 8, 490, he experienced a dream involving Saint Michael. "By this sign, I am watching over and guarding [this] place,"[8] the angel told him in the vision. The grotto was destined to become a holy site in the region, but Bishop Laurence was still uncertain — in spite of the vision from the archangel himself.

Shortly thereafter, the region was in the midst of attacking pagan forces from Naples, called the Neapolitans. This invasion of Monte Gargano was followed by an earthquake, lightning, and heavenly-sent arrows mowing down the enemy. Footprints of Michael himself were claimed to be imprinted into the rock of the grotto, rock deemed holy, indeed, "not made by human hands." The date of victory over the Neapolitans was September 29. It is believed Michael and the angels themselves consecrated the grotto on September 29, 493, before eyewitnesses including bishops. They found in place an altar covered by a red cloth and a crucifix set upon it. Pieces of the altar cloth relic, as will be seen in chapter 5, were later sent to other places of dedication to Saint Michael to unite them with Gargano.

In any event, Pope Gelasius I (492–496) approved the sanctuary as a basilica, called the "Celestial Basilica." At last, Bishop Laurence was not uncertain any longer. Nearly two centuries later, another victory by the Lombards over the Greek Neapolitans transpired on May 8, 663, the anniversary of Michael's apparition to Bishop Laurence.

Another apparition of Michael is said to have occurred in 1656 when a plague ravaged the region. Bishop Alfonso Puccinelli appealed to Michael for some kind of supernatural intervention, if it be God's will, through prayer and fasting. At dawn on September 22, Michael appeared to the bishop while he prayed in his room, instructing him to engrave a symbol on the grotto stones:

S. ✠ M.

Bishop Puccinelli was then to bless the stones and deliver them to the people of the region. Whoever possessed such a stone would be spared from the pestilence. Soon after, the plague passed over. In gratitude, Bishop Puccinelli ordered a monument constructed and placed in the town square, the inscription reading:

> To the Prince of the Angels
> Conqueror of the Plague
> Patron and Guardian
> we place this monument
> in eternal gratitude
> Alfonso Puccinelli
> 1656[9]

On the Church calendar, May 8 became designated as the feast of the Apparition of St. Michael, while September 29, the dedication of the grotto in 493, became Saint Michael's own feast day, Michaelmas Day.

The sanctuary to Saint Michael on Monte Gargano, the oldest shrine dedicated to the archangel in western Christendom, was so venerated and considered so holy that Saint Francis of Assisi, traveling to the site on pilgrimage, considered himself unworthy to enter the cave. Given its proximity to the port of Manfredonia, Monte Gargano was also the site of a popular pilgrim stop for crusaders, particularly those from Normandy, en route to the Holy Land. Other saints and popes have traversed the hilltop as pilgrims, including Pope Saint John Paul II in 1987. As detailed in chapter 5, the holy cave where the bull so long ago was found kneeling became one of seven sanctuaries spanning thousands of kilometers to comprise what is known as Saint Michael's Sword.

Michael in the Eternal City

The immediate popularity of Monte Gargano's cavernous sanctuary quickly spread. At Rome, Gregory the Great reigned as pope from 590–604. It was the time of the so-called Dark Ages, the period from Rome's fall in A.D. 476 until the last century of the first millennium. With Constantine having relocated the center of the empire east to

Byzantium a century and a half earlier, the only one left in Rome with any kind of authority was the Roman pontiff.

Pope Gregory's immediate predecessor, Pelagius II, had succumbed to the plague. With little material aid left to help the Roman people, Gregory had recourse to spiritual sustenance. On the morning of April 25, 590, the pope led a penitential procession through the plague-infested Eternal City whose population had been decimated. On the modern Church calendar, April 25 is known as the feast of Saint Mark, but that particular day initially became the date designated by Pope Gregory as the Greater Litanies, an annual procession of great grandeur. "Pale-faced, emaciated, and clad in deepest mourning, the people moved slowly through the desolate streets ... scarcely a sound was heard save the tramp of feet, and sobs and cries for mercy, and over all the doleful chant of the Kyrie Eleison."[10]

On this April 25, however, as the Pope carried the Holy Icon of Our Lady of Santa Maria Maggiore, some people in the procession were so sick that they collapsed. While the procession crossed the Aelian Bridge over the Tiber, in the shadow of Hadrian's tomb — the massive, imposing fortress built for the Roman Emperor Hadrian in A.D. 139 — a heavenly choir, intoning the *Regina Coeli*, directed the procession's gaze skyward:

Regina caeli, laetare, alleluia;
Quia quem meruisti portare, alleluia,
Resurrexit, sicut dixit, alleluia ...

To which Pope Gregory responded: "*Ora pro nobis Deum, alleluia!*"

(In English, "Queen of heaven, rejoice, alleluia! The son you merited to bear, alleluia, has risen as he said, alleluia. Pray to God for us, alleluia.")

According to *The Golden Legend*, an immensely popular collection of stories gathered by chronicler-priest (and archbishop of Genoa) Jacobus Voragine (1228–1298), Gregory then saw above the mausoleum the glorious and fearless Saint Michael clean blood from his sword and sheathe it. It is believed the plague ended at that moment.

Saint Ado of Vienne (800–875) documented that Gregory's successor, Pope Boniface IV (reigned 608–615), installed a chapel atop Hadrian's Mausoleum in thanksgiving for the miracle of April 25, 590. The structure itself eventually became a fortress for the popes, complete with a celebrated eight hundred meter elevated secret passageway, the Passetto di Borgo, linking the fort to the Vatican. Not long afterward, a statue of Saint Michael was installed at the summit of the mausoleum in the spot where Gregory saw the archangel. The statue itself has gone through several iterations over time, and the current one has been in place since 1753, in the time of Pope Benedict XIV.[11] It was renamed Castel Sant'Angelo, and remains a powerful fixture of the Roman landscape to this day.

Over the centuries, dozens of shrines, churches, and towns populated the map of Italy in veneration to Saint Michael, from Monte San Michele in Sicily to Dusino San Michele in Piedmont. Stories of apparitions, interventions, and miracles are bountiful; they are part of Italian Catholicism. When Italians emigrated to America, they brought their devotion to the archangel with them by building, for instance, Saint Michael's in New Haven, Connecticut; Saint Michael's in Chicago's Italian neighborhood; and Saint Michael's Church in Portland's Little Italy. In these and in many more instances, we see that the archangel continues his protective service to the people of God as begun in the time of the Israelites.

In time, Saint Michael was named protector of Vatican City on July 5, 2013, by Pope Francis. That both Pope Francis and Pope Emeritus Benedict XVI attended the dedication ceremony of a Saint Michael statue in the Vatican Gardens in July 2013 emphasized the prime importance of Saint Michael's role as not just a guardian of nations, but also of the Church as a whole.

But we must now depart the rustic Italian landscape. A new kingdom fell in love with the prince of the heavenly hosts — the eldest daughter of the Church and that most Christian country: Catholic France.

Jeanne d'Arc / Eugène Romain Thirion, Public domain

4
Protector of France

Today, there is little memory of France's majestic Catholic roots — only 4.5 percent of French Catholics attend Mass.[1] While Holy Mother Church survived, the detrimental effects of the French Revolution (1789–1799) thoroughly reshaped the role of Catholicism in the former passionately Catholic country. Those effects are still felt today. France was fundamentally transformed after the Revolution, infused with the philosophy of the Enlightenment, positivism, and, ultimately, relativism. Yet once we dig past the overgrowth and the ruins of the Revolution, we can still find the Catholic soul of that most Christian country. And in doing so, we find the enduring presence of one beloved figure, Saint Michael the Archangel, who again and again emerges during France's darkest hours.

Foundations of Faith

The foundations of France's vibrant Catholicism were laid in a seemingly innocuous event: a baptism at the end of the fifth century. King Clovis I was only fifteen when he succeeded his father, Childeric, as Merovingian king of the Franks in A.D. 481. Clovis spent the next thirty years until his death subjugating regional subkings. By 508, Clovis ruled all Franks under one kingdom, Francia, and made Paris his primary residence.

The impetus for his baptism stemmed from the tireless example of his wife, Clotilde. Gregory of Tours documented that Clotilde would not give up her quiet evangelization of Clovis. And, as with many men of influence throughout history, Clovis finally heard God's voice where it mattered most — on the battlefield. In the Battle of Tolbiac against the Alamani, a collection of Germanic tribes, the Franks were surrounded and bracing for defeat. Amid the carnage around him, the normally reserved Clovis was finally broken. Gregory reports:

> [Clovis] raised his eyes to heaven, and with remorse in his heart he burst into tears and cried: 'Jesus Christ, whom Clotilde asserts to be the son of the living God, who art said to give aid to those in distress, and to bestow victory on those who hope in thee, I beseech the glory of thy aid, with the vow that if thou wilt grant me victory over these enemies, and I shall know that power which she says that people dedicated in thy name have had from thee, I will believe in thee and be baptized in thy name. For I have invoked my own gods but, as I find, they have withdrawn from aiding me; and therefore I believe that they possess no power, since they do not help those who obey them. I now call upon thee, I desire to believe thee only let me be rescued from my adversaries.[2]

The tide of the battle soon shifted in favor of Clovis and the Franks, and at the moment victory was secured, Clovis ceased any further unnecessary bloodshed. He was baptized soon thereafter, on Christmas Day, 496. The Bishop of Reims, Remigius, administered the sacrament. In time, Clovis's wife became recognized as Saint Clotilde, and Remigius as Saint Remigius.

Charlemagne and Saint Michael

Over the centuries following Clovis's conversion, the church in Francia continued to flourish. In the late first millennium, the local Church was in need of reform, and was brought back to fervor by the missionary bishop Saint Boniface. Boniface had the support of one Charles Martel, grandfather of the first Holy Roman Emperor, Charlemagne.

When he came to power, not only was Charlemagne aware of the growing spiritual vibrancy of the people under his domain — inspired by the missionary work of Boniface and his disciples — but also, like many others in this time, he was occupied by the concept of the end times. The imagery and language of the Book of Revelation was foremost in his mind. Charlemagne possessed an acute awareness of Michael's import in the cosmic struggle against Satan. As Charlemagne grew in temporal stature in both the East and the West, he sought to construct his palace at Aachen as a deliberate evocation of the Heavenly Jerusalem as depicted in Revelation.[3]

A close confidant of Charlemagne was a Benedictine monk of Saint-Mihiel Abbey, Smaragdus. It was Smaragdus who, at the behest of Charlemagne, composed a letter to Pope Leo III supporting the Roman Church's position regarding the *Filioque* — a theological matter of great debate between East and West Christianity that attested the Holy Spirit proceeds from both the Father and the Son. In time, this distinction, among other tensions, led to the formal split known as the Great Schism in 1054.

The influence of Saint Michael on Charlemagne manifested itself in other concrete and far-reaching ways:

- After Charlemagne's conquest of the Lombards, the intense devotion to Saint Michael that had developed at Monte Gargano in Apulia spread north. Charlemagne was advised by an Englishman named Cathwulf to not discourage the cult to Michael and denounce it as something unique to the Lombards, but rather publicly celebrate Saint Michael in the kingdom.

- Charlemagne, in his edict *Admonitio generalis* in 789, established the feast of Saint Michael, September 29 (Michaelmas Day), to be observed throughout the whole of Francia.
- For October 16, the feast of the Dedication of Mont-Saint-Michel, the magnificent shrine to Saint Michael we will discuss further in chapter 6, Charlemagne approved this preface to the sacramentary for Frankish liturgies: "It is proper … that on this day we proclaim the merits of Saint Michael the Archangel. For however much we are to venerate all the angels who stand in the presence of your Majesty, it is proper that in this celestial order the warrior (angel) deserves the first rank."[4]
- During Charlemagne's rule, battle standards were created featuring an image of Michael with the Latin words *Patronus et Princeps Imperii Galliarum*, Patron and Prince of the Empire of the Gauls.[5]

Additionally, Saint Michael was also evoked at Charlemagne's coronation as *Imperator Augustus*, Holy Roman Emperor, by Pope Saint Leo III at Saint Peter's in Rome on Christmas Day in the year 800. Even before the coronation Charlemagne was a hallowed figure. Bold lyrics in the Carolingian *laudes regiae*, the royal hymns, raised Charlemagne to the heights of the heavenly exalted, after the apostles and sainted popes and before the Blessed Virgin Mary, archangels, Saint John, and Saint Stephen.[6]

Michael's influence is again evident in the work of Alcuin, a priest and chief scholar in the school at Charlemagne's palace in Aachen, when he composed *Sequentia de sancto Michaele*, citing Michael as "chief citizen of heaven" and included these stirring words: "You, when you scattered the fierce dragon with your strong hand, plucked many souls from his jaws."[7] Alcuin ends by directly beseeching Michael: "Hear us, Michael, greatest angel, come down here a little from your heavenly throne, to bring us the help and solace of the mercy of the Lord." One can be sure that if the king and emperor frequently sought out the intercession and protection of Saint Michael, his subjects across Francia and the vast Holy Roman Empire were doing the same.

Saint Michael and Saint Joan

Many centuries later, Saint Joan of Arc (1412–1431) cannot be separated from her devotion to Saint Michael, whose voice (along those with Saint Catherine of Alexandria and Saint Margaret of Antioch) Joan claimed to have inspired her astounding and unlikely military successes. The Hundred Years' War (1337–1475), a series of conflicts between England and France, was still raging when Joan entered the fray. France was desperately looking for an intervention. The vast majority of the war occurred on French soil, striking down generations of a people already crippled by the Black Plague. The English occupied Paris by 1429. Hope of successfully defending France seemed dismal.

Saint Joan was born in Domremy in the Duchy of Bar, not far from the Benedictine abbey of Saint-Mihiel. Joan was twelve or thirteen when she had her first visions of Saint Michael, Saint Catherine, and Saint Margaret. Later, she told her interrogators that when first encountering Saint Michael, she was so sure it was he simply because he announced himself quite clearly: "I am Michael, the protector of France." This description of his identity stirred something within Joan, who was then commanded by the saints to personally involve herself in combating the English. Her objective was clear: to lead the dauphin, Charles VII, into the Notre-Dame Cathedral at Reims, the historic site for the coronation of French kings, and to see him crowned. That Joan was so young and without any military experience whatsoever was evidently not a concern to her saintly guides — or to Joan herself.

Four years later, this obscure young peasant commanded the successful French siege at Orléans, about 120 kilometers southwest of Paris. The English surrendered on May 8, 1429 — the same day as the feast of the Apparition of Saint Michael on Monte Gargano. Another successful and important battle for French forces led by Joan, the Battle of Patay, was fought the following month on June 18. In Constantinople's Church of Saint Julian in the Orthodox east, June 18 was traditionally regarded as one of the feasts venerating Saint Michael.

By July, the army arrived in Reims, where Charles VII was duly crowned on July 18, fulfilling Joan's original mission when first encountering the visions of her beloved saints on her family farm years earlier. But Joan did not stop in Reims, and continued on to free Paris, the heart of France, from English hands. Ultimately, however, the Duke of Burgundy, an English loyalist, captured Joan and she was brought to Rouen to face her accusers. It was an Inquisitorial trial, a textbook show trial, and one decidedly pro-English.

Joan's eventual trial and execution occurred in Rouen, in Normandy, then also under English control. But there was one part of Normandy that had not yet fallen into English hands over the course of the seemingly endless war: the spiritual fortress of Mont-Saint-Michel (see chapter 5). Charles VII, no more than a few years older than Joan, designed a new battle standard for his weary troops: Saint Michael, sword unsheathed from scabbard, looming over the desperate figure of the devil.[8] To Charles VII and the French, he was the archangel on whom they pinned all their fleeting hopes.

Even in prison, Saint Michael did not abandon Joan: "I heard his voice yesterday and today, in the morning and at vespers, and at the Ave Maria, and I have heard him much more often," Joan testified. Under the covers of exhaustion and immense pressure, Joan signed a confession renouncing her actions — only to retract it the next day. Found guilty of heresy, Joan of Arc was burned alive at the stake in Rouen on May 30, 1431. But Joan was canonized by the Catholic Church as a saint by Pope Benedict XV on May 16, 1920.

Those who condemned her as a heretic are forgotten to history, and now Saint Joan stands with Saint Michael as protector of the country to which she gave her life, France.

Military Order of Saint Michael

Louis XI, the son of Charles VII who succeeded his father as king of France, instituted the Military Order of Saint Michael on August 1, 1469, in Amboise, just outside Tours in the Loire Valley. The Order of Saint Michael was a chivalric order and stood as the highest order in France for nearly one hundred years. Chivalric orders were immensely popular in the Middle Ages. Membership prompted loyalty to king and kingdom through the intercession of a particular saint or devotion, such as France's Order of the Star named after the Star of Bethlehem, or the Order of Saint George, dedicated to the Trinity with particular devotion to the patron of chivalry, Saint George.

Every member of the Order of Saint Michael received a gold badge showing Saint Michael atop Mont-Saint-Michel, doing battle with the serpent over Atlantic waters. Indeed, the order's motto read *Immensi Tremor Oceani* ("the tremor of the immense ocean"). King Louis XI actually intended on identifying Mont-Saint-Michel as the Order's chapel, but ultimately deemed it too far from Paris. The Order's gold badge hung from a gold collar of scallop shells, a fascinating inclusion; even today, pilgrims along the Santiago de Compostela will notice the shell is the pilgrim badge for the Way of Saint James.

As it happened, however, the Order of Saint Michael was abolished by Louis XVI in June 1790, under pressure from the vehement anti-clericalism and anti-Catholicism sentiment of the French Revolution. While it was temporarily restored in the nineteenth century, it was short-lived, and has since disappeared like so much of France's Catholic past.

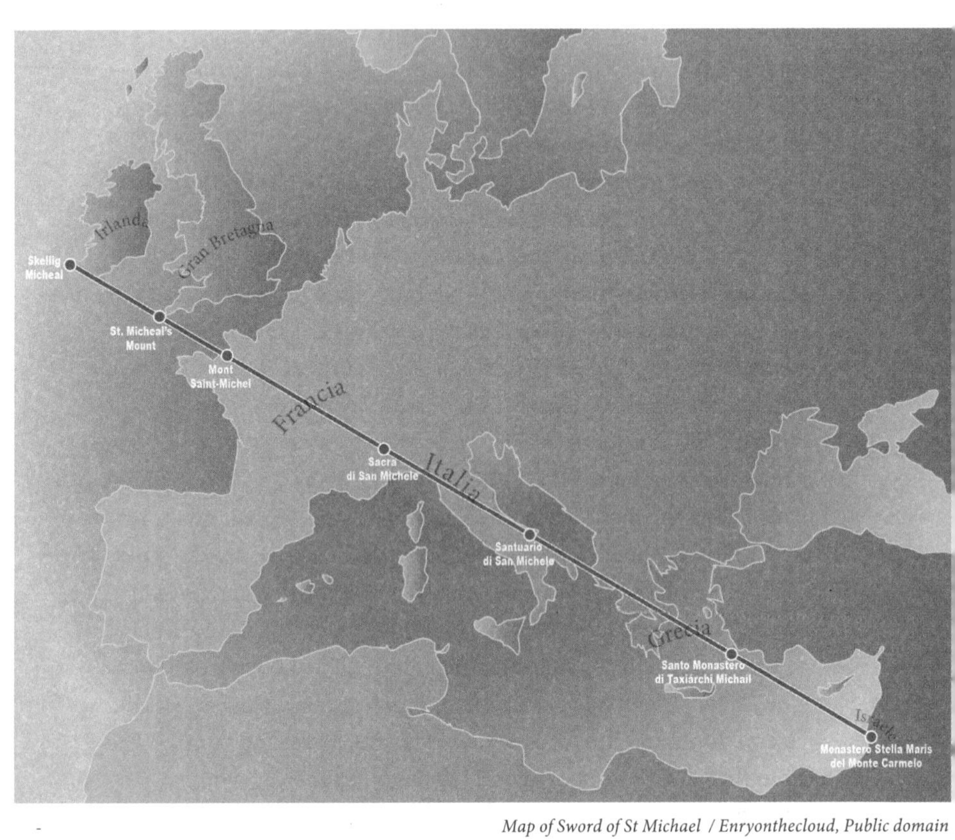

Map of Sword of St Michael / Enryonthecloud, Public domain

5
The Sword of Saint Michael

The sanctuaries dedicated to Saint Michael on Monte Gargano in Apulia and Mont-Saint-Michel in Normandy inspired reverent devotion to Michael across the centuries. These eye-popping structures, wholly otherworldly, not only withstood the march of time and the natural elements but also defied attacking armies seeking to dismantle these spiritual beacons of hope in one way or another. Mont-Saint-Michel and Monte Gargano are about 1,800 kilometers apart, and both are situated near bodies of water, a testament to longstanding invocation by seafarers to Michael. But what is remarkable about the location of these spiritual fortresses, built centuries apart, is that a straight line drawn between the two calls attention to more sanctuaries dedicated to Saint Michael situated along the same axis. Known as the "Sword of Saint Michael," this geographic line stretches from the windswept isles of Ireland to the Holy Land of Israel.

Skellig Michael in Ireland; Saint Michael's Mount in Cornwall, England; Mont-Saint-Michel in Normandy; Sacra di San Michele in Turin, Italy; Monte Gargano in Apulia; Archangel Michael of Panormitis Monastery in Greece; and Stella Maris Monastery in Haifa, Israel, all combine to form this so-called Sword of Saint Michael. This nickname derived from the legend that the line represents Saint Michael delivering the decisive blow that hurtled Satan from heaven. "I saw Satan fall like lightning from heaven," we recall Christ's assertion in the Gospel of Luke (10:18). Each of the seven sanctuaries supplanted old pagan temples and shrines designed to specifically welcome the sunset of the summer solstice. Christ, the Son of God, was now the focus of worship through devotion to Saint Michael. Remarkably, the formation of this sword of Saint Michael was utterly unintentional. But as Pope John Paul II once said, "In the designs of Providence there are no mere coincidences."

The uncanny alignment of these sanctuaries has captured the attention of not a few individuals, intrigued by whether their geographical placement was intentional or coincidental, if not providential. Among these is a physicist at the Institute of Theoretical Physics in Heidelberg, Germany, Luca Amendola. A native of Rome, Amendola is also an astronomer at the Italian National Institute for Astrophysics. After the Star Wars movie company announced production would film on Skellig Michael, Amendola published an essay, "Luke Skywalker and the St. Michael Axis." In the piece, he notes that two Frenchman, the Richer brothers, detected the alignment of shrines all positioned on the same axis. Originally, Jean Richer's work in 1967 addressed the alignment of ancient Greek temples. But, Amendola notes, it was Jean's brother, Lucien Richer, who discovered the lines went further, which included what constitutes "the sword of Saint Michael."[1]

Skellig Michael

When the film trailer to the motion picture *Star Wars: The Last Jedi* debuted in 2017, viewers were captivated by the stirring shots of a verdant, rocky island in the middle of the sea. In the movie,

Skellig Michael / KedilerNicole, CC BY-SA (https://creativecommons.org/licenses/by-sa/4.0)

it is known as Ahch-To, the Jedi hermitage for Luke Skywalker. The popularity of the film generated great interest in the real-life island, with tours surging in the wake of the film's release.

Located off the southwestern coast of Kerry in the Republic of Ireland, 270 kilometers from the nearest major city of Cork, Skellig Michael receives its name from the Gaelic meaning "splinter of stone," describing the view of the island's rock formation. Legends from Irish mythology mention the island as the site of shipwrecks, burials, and a place of refuge.

Augustinian monks inhabited the island certainly by the eighth century, though the traditional founding of the island monastery is credited to Saint Finnian of Clonard (A.D. 470–549), a father of Irish monasticism. An ancient account, *Libellus de Fundacione Ecclesie Consecrati Petri*, places Saint Patrick on the island in his final bouts against the snakes and demons of Ireland.

A record notating the death of one "Aedh of Scelic-Mhichil" indicates the name Skellig Michael was in use before 1044,[2] and thus Saint Michael was already the patron of the island monks. A church dedicated to Saint Michael was installed in the monastery, a detail mentioned by Giraldus Cambrensis in the late 1100s. This Irish chronicler further noted a miracle at this remote monastery church of Saint Michael:

> There is an island with a church dedicated to Saint Michael, famed for its orthodox sanctity from very ancient times. There is a stone outside the porch of this church, on the right hand, and partly fixed in the wall, with a hollow in its surface, which, every morning, through the merits of the saint to whom the church is dedicated, is filled with as much wine as will conveniently suffice for the service of the masses on the day ensuing, according to the number of the priests there who have to celebrate them.[3]

By the end of the sixteenth century, after Queen Elizabeth dissolved monasteries as a consequence of the Desmond Rebellion in 1578, the monks abandoned Skellig Michael.[4] Thanks to the Irish Office of Public Works and eventually UNESCO protecting the island as a World Heritage Site, visitors can explore the mystical landscape of Skellig Michael as they begin their spiritual pilgrimage along the route of the Sword of Saint Michael.

Mount Saint Michael

Continuing along the Sword, we arrive at Mount Saint Michael in Cornwall, England. Evoking both the rocky greenery of Skellig Michael and the breathtaking architecture of Mont-Saint-Michel on the opposite side of the Channel, Mount Saint Michael is accessible by a thin natural causeway, similar to its counterpart in Normandy. The island is situated 365 meters from the shore of Mount's Bay on the Cornwall coast of the English Channel, almost 400 kilometers southeast of Skellig Michael, and 300 kilometers across the Channel to Mont-Saint-Michel.

Its distinctive similarities to Mont-Saint-Michel are not entirely

St. Michael's Mount Cornwall / Chensiyuan ,CC BY-SA (https://creativecommons.org/licenses/by-sa/4.0)

accidental: in the time of King Saint Edward the Confessor (1003–1066), the last king of the House of Wessex before the Norman Invasion, Count Robert of Mortain donated the site to the Benedictines of Mont-Saint-Michel. Naturally, Saint Michael was chosen as the spiritual protector of this abbey as well, his patronage now flanking both sides of the English Channel.

During the Lancastrian stage of the Hundred Years' War, in the decade before the rise of Joan of Arc, King Henry V of England dissolved the priory of Saint Michael and took over the island from ecclesiastical management. Nevertheless, it continued to be a popular pilgrimage site over the centuries, spurred by a long-standing indulgence granted by Pope Gregory VI in 1046.[5]

The stone church of St. Michael, dating to the 1100s, holds Anglican services each weekend in the seasonal months.[6] The modern-day proprietors of Saint Michael's Mount promote the sacred grounds as an opportunity for tourism, hospitality, and events. While much of the landscape of ancient Christendom —

former shrines, abandoned churches, monasteries — have been repurposed from their spiritual roots, these sanctuaries to Saint Michael still remain in the public consciousness, as if Michael is patiently waiting to once again lead people out of spiritual darkness into the light of God.

Saint Michael's Mount is also a point along another geographic spiritual path involving the archangel and England. From Cornwall to the Great Yarmouth in Norfolk on the eastern tip of England, sites in honor of Saint Michael or Saint George are aligned along the Beltane sunrise path. This solar phenomenon was commemorated annually by a pagan Gaelic event celebrating the halfway point between the spring equinox and the summer solstice. Often such an event would occur on May 8 — the feast of the apparition of Saint Michael at Monte Gargano.[7]

One of these sites is Glastonbury Tor, a landmark in Celtic mythology and the purported burial place of Joseph of Arimathea in Arthurian lore. At the top of Tor Hill is a simple, roofless tower. Its name is Saint Michael's Tower, the sole surviving remnant of the medieval Saint Michael Church. Other sanctuaries devoted to Saint Michael along this axis are St. Michael de Rupe in Brentor and St. Michael's Church in Burrow Mump, the last point before Glastonbury Tor.

Mont-Saint-Michel

Situated in the northwest region of France is Normandy, long a place of great historical importance. King Clovis consolidated most of it during his reign, a land where Celtic tribes inhabited pockets of the region long before the Roman conquest. The Vikings launched devastating invasions on both Normandy and neighboring Brittany. It is home to the County of Anjou and its Angevin Empire that produced Eleanor of Aquitaine and rivaled the power of the King of France. England itself temporarily controlled Normandy in the Hundred Years' War, out of vengeance for the Duke of Normandy, William the Conqueror,

Mont Saint Michel / Amaustan, CC BY-SA (https://creativecommons.org/licenses/by-sa/4.0)

sailing across the English Channel in the Norman Conquest of England. Normandy's beaches were ground zero for the June 6, 1944, D-Day operation that turned the tide in World War II.

The area is both beautiful and desolate; high tides and intemperate weather are the norms. It is the perfect place for a monastery to Saint Michael.

The lone surviving narrative of the founding of this most impressive monastery is the hagiographic ninth century work, *Revelatio Ecclesiae Sancti Michaelis*. A summary of the account is as follows:[8] In the time of King Childebert III (c. 708), Saint Michael appeared to Bishop Aubert of the Diocese of Avranches three times requesting the building of sanctuary in his name in the manner as at Monte Gargano. Like the Bishop of Siponto, Aubert hesitated — until in his third apparition Michael nudged Aubert on the side of the head with his finger, so much so it left a dent, or so goes the legend.[9] To this day, Saint-Gervais Basilica in Avranches houses a relic of Aubert's skull, with visible indentation.

Michael instructed Aubert to build the sanctuary atop Mont

Tombe, a rocky islet one kilometer off the Normandy coast, accessible by a natural causeway at low tide. The church's construction proceeded not without a gift from the abbot of Mount Gargano, to establish a confraternity between the two shrines. The abbot gave two relics left by Michael at Gargano: a piece of the red cloth from the mystical Gargano altar, and a piece of marble on which the archangel had stood. The *Revelatio* then details numerous miracles that transpired because of these relics. Finally, with twelve Canons Regular established at the simple monastery, Mont-Saint-Michel was dedicated on October 16.

To the medieval Catholic imagination attuned to the mysteries of the Faith, a desolate island sanctuary off the desert coast, somehow both inviting and intimidating, was a powerful image that evoked images of the Christian life: everything from desert asceticism to the fishermen who became fishers of men (cf. Mk 1:17). Speculation also ensued on how the island had formed off the coast. A hypothesis was hatched that a quasi-mythical forest named Scissy occupied the bay, until either a tremendous earthquake, tidal wave, or storm broke the island off the mainland. It was also suggested Christian monks — namely, Saint Pair and Saint Scubillon — inhabited Mont Tombe even before Aubert's apparitions of Michael.

Whatever its origins, Mont-Saint-Michel defied all weather conditions and assaults from warring forces. It became a major pilgrimage site, and underwent modifications and increased fortifications during the medieval era, much of which are still seen today. Though it is now geared for the plethora of tourists intermingled with the devout pilgrim, it is firmly imprinted as a site wondrous to behold across cultures and nations. Viewers of *The Return of the King*, the concluding film in *The Lord of the Rings* trilogy, will find the mountainous city of Minas Tirith resembling the sanctuary of Mont-Saint-Michel.

Sacra di San Michele

From Mont-Saint-Michel and slicing across France through the

Sacra di San Michele / Elio Pallard, CC BY-SA (https://creativecommons.org/licenses/by-sa/4.0)

Cottian Alps, we next come to Sacra di San Michele in Piedmont's Val di Susa, thirty kilometers from the Cathedral of San Giovanni Battista, home of the Shroud of Turin. This jaw-dropping site, Italy's northernmost sanctuary dedicated to Saint Michael, defies description. Looming nearly eight hundred meters above the town of Sant'Ambrogio di Torino on Monte Pirchiriano, Sacra di San Michele was yet another sanctuary to Saint Michael established by the Benedictines.

To Milanese poet Clemente Rebora (1885–1957), Sacra di San Michele was perched on a "summit steeped in holiness." Tradition holds Saint Giovanni Vincenzo, archbishop of Ravenna, took up life as a hermit in the complex that eventually became known as Sacra di San Michele. Saint Giovanni Vincenzo is still recognized as the patron saint of Sant'Ambrogio di Torino. Tradition also tells it was Saint Michael's urging that prompted Giovanni to envision building Sacra di San Michele. The Benedictines set the foundation for Sacra di San Michele in the 980s, and the stone abbey facade, dating to the twelfth century, towers forty meters high.

Monte Gargano / Cesare Nebbia, CC0

Archangel Michael of Panormitis Monastery

After visiting the Sanctuary of Saint Michael on Monte Gargano in Apulia, which we have already covered in chapter 4, we continue our journey southeast to a fourth island sanctuary. In Greece, the influence of Christianity over the centuries is evident in the vast number of Greek Orthodox monasteries that populate the lush landscape.

Archangel Michael of Panormitis Monastery is one of those monasteries. Situated on an island like most of the sanctuaries that make up the Sword of Saint Michael, this monastery is located on the island of Symi, part of the Dodecanese islands in the southeastern Aegean Sea near Rhode. Panormitis Monastery is located directly on the sea front in a cove within the tiny village of Panormitis, population 2,580. Here, pilgrim and tourist alike are immediately drawn to the monastery's bell tower, its structure evoking the similarly styled Basilica of Our Lady of the Rosary in Fatima, Portugal. Like other sanctuaries in our journey along Saint Michael's Sword, the monastery at Panormitis was built upon a former pagan temple, one dedicated to the Greek god Apollo.

It is not exactly known when Panormitis Monastery was founded, but it is believed to have been around A.D. 450. While that date is uncertain, evidence of the monastery's presence at the time of the fall of Constantinople by the Ottoman Turks in 1453 is far better known. The feast day of the Monastery is November 8, the same day Michael is venerated in the Eastern Church. In Symi it is marked by a solemn procession through the village led by the Greek Orthodox bishop of the region. And contained within the monastery grounds is a unique image: a silver and gold icon of Saint Michael. For the November 8 feast day, the icon is removed from the monastery and is included in the procession through Panormitis.

Indeed, Saint Michael is not only the patron of Symi but also the protector of sailors throughout the whole of the Dodecanese, yet another example of Saint Michael as refuge for those sailing the seas.

Taxiarchis Monastery / Aleksei m, CC BY-SA (https://creativecommons.org/licenses/by-sa/4.0)

Stella Maris Monastery

Our pilgrimage along the Sword of Saint Michael concludes after venturing over 4,000 kilometers to finally reaching, appropriately, the Holy Land. Located in Haifa, the promontory 150 kilometers north of Jerusalem on the Mediterranean, this particular monastery is traditionally included in the Sword of Saint Michael despite being less devoted specifically to Saint Michael and more a nexus of Catholic themes.

First, Stella Maris Monastery is named after the Mother of God, the Star of the Sea (*Stella Maris*), the one before whom Michael and all the angels and saints bow. Built on the grotto believed to be the home of the prophet Elijah, Stella Maris is a Carmelite monastery, an order founded on Haifa's Mount Carmel during the period of the Latin Kingdom of Jerusalem of the crusading era. Third, Mount Carmel is the site detailed in the Old Testament's Book of Kings where Elijah triumphs over the prophets of Baal, ultimately ending a catastrophic drought when his burnt sacrifice is favored over those of Baal's prophets (see 1 Kgs 18:20–40). Elijah's directive to the people — "If the LORD is God, follow him; if Baal, follow him" — echoes the motto of Saint Michael: *Quis ut Deus?* "Who is like God?" This is the whole theme of Elijah's prophetic witness, whose name in Hebrew means "My God is Yahweh." In the following chapter, an unnamed angel brings food to Elijah (1 Kgs 19:5). Though the Book of Kings does not mention the angel by name, the apocryphal work Apocalypse of Elijah is structured around Elijah receiving revelations from an angel, Saint Michael.

Stella Maris underwent periods of ruin and restoration throughout its existence. Napoleon's troops wreaked havoc on the church in 1799, and the Ottoman chieftain Abdullah Pasha demolished the church completely. What is seen today was built in 1836, and is considered the spiritual center for all Carmelites around the world.

Places of Pilgrimage

In his book *Jesus of Nazareth,* Pope Benedict XVI writes, "God ... revealed his face only in Israel, even though he was also honored among the pagans in various shadowy guises." The shrines and monasteries along this "sword of Saint Michael" may have been locations originally for pagan purposes, but they transformed into holy places for the Most High. In honoring Saint Michael, the angel so loyal to the Holy Trinity, these sanctuaries testify that the God of Jesus Christ is the one, true God.

From the Irish isle to Israel, each of these sites is physically unique, but Saint Michael links them all and directs them toward the Heavenly Jerusalem. Each of these sanctuaries testifies to the endurance of the Faith in season and out of season. All vocations, from seafarers to cloistered religious, find a common devotion in these places. Their historical context merged with their spiritual significance to open up new ways of our understanding of history and the customs of different cultures. When seen with the eyes of faith, the past no longer is remote and irrelevant. How can we not be inspired by the ambition of our ancestors in faith to honor the living God?

In this way, our journey along the sword of Saint Michael instills a renewed sense of pilgrimage. Certainly, contemporary Catholicism strongly promotes pilgrimages, such as the Holy Land, the Way of Saint James, or the World Youth Days. While we might be unable to physically embark on a "sword of Saint Michael pilgrimage," the importance and legacy of these sanctuaries challenge us that when we do venture elsewhere, our Catholic Faith is likely to be found just around a corner or across a bridge. Perhaps we might begin to look at ourselves as pilgrims first, and then tourists. Doing so might just increase our own connection to our spiritual past while instilling a new sense of responsibility in preserving these sites of faith for the future.

Retablo of the Archangel St. Michael/San Miguel Arcangel, 1840 / José Rafael Aragón, Public domain

6
Saint Michael in the Nineteenth Century

By the time of the 1800s, Christendom, as it had been known for hundreds of years, had fragmented. Catholic identity was less a priority for the ruling class; the French Revolution of 1789 was only the first in a series of revolts in France; other monarchies and royal families also were toppled in the 1800s, such as the Catholic Habsburgs in Austria, the dissolution of New Spain in the Americas, and the May Revolution in Argentina. Napoleon effectively kidnapped and imprisoned two popes, Pius VI and Pius VII, seeking to eradicate the papacy's influence — if not perhaps the papacy itself. Italy's eventual unification in 1870 isolated the pope's temporal power to the Vatican alone.

When a nation's Catholicism is no longer a guarantee in the life of its people, two things occur: the right to practice a religion is determined by government, and the Catholic Faith must compete against other ideologies. Such ideologies themselves often become a form of religion. At last, Christianity became something to suppress and replace.

In the post-Enlightenment period, Marxism, communism, socialism, masonry, positivism, liberalism, modernism, and relativism all contended as attractive alternatives to the one, true Catholic Faith. At this critical juncture, the Church was gifted with only two popes for nearly sixty years, Pope Pius IX (1846–1878) and Pope Leo XIII (1878–1903). At this time, Saint Michael again did battle, so much so that Pius IX noted that Saint Michael was the most able of God's messengers to eradicate the evil of those ideologies seeking to abolish Catholicism. As we will see in this chapter, both Leo XIII and Pius IX can be rightly deemed "the two popes of Saint Michael." Their vigilance in combating evil during both of their pontificates by summoning Michael's protection influenced their successors and helped establish a renewed devotion to the archangel.

Venerable Philomena de Santa Colomba

A holy woman recognized as Venerable by Pope Leo XIII was instrumental in instilling devotion to Saint Michael in the nineteenth century. Philomena Ferrer was born in 1841 in Móra d'Ebre, a small village of Catalonia. At eighteen, Philomena entered the convent of the Minims near Barcelona. Though Philomena died in 1868 at only age twenty-seven, her devotion to Saint Michael occurred at such a time when the archangel returned to Catholic consciousness, and whose impact reached the highest levels of spiritual leadership.

Private revelations and profound spiritual insights characterized Philomena's meteoric life. One early vision is preserved:

> While the devil was hovering about me, I felt myself touched very gently on my right shoulder, and, turning round, I saw a most beautiful angel, who invited me to follow him into the smaller choir, next to that of the community. It seemed to me that I obeyed neither against my will nor with my own free-will, as I was no longer mistress of my faculties. On en-

> tering the place I saw Jesus and Mary. They spoke to me tenderly, and invited me to rest in their sweet company after the fatigue which I had experienced in praying for the soul of whom I have spoken above, and also from the assaults and attacks of the devil. I remained still with astonishment, not knowing what I ought to do; when it seemed to me that the Mother and the Son made me taste some exquisite food, and drink a celestial and wholly divine liquid. The taste of this food made me take a disgust to all earthly nourishment, and at the same time that it left in my soul an ineffaceable sweetness.[1]

Philomena experienced visions not unlike those granted to the peasant children of Fátima in the subsequent century: images of a world in chaos, with three-fourths of the world succumbing to plagues and violence. One vision even involved the pope himself, but Philomena was assured in the vision the pope would not be forced to flee from Rome, even if a nation would soon occupy the Eternal City in her own lifetime.

A year before Philomena's death, Saint Michael appeared to the young woman in another vision, instructing her: "Make known to men the great power which I have with the Most High. Tell them to ask of me all they wish. Tell them that my power in favor of those devoted to me is without limit. Make known my greatness."

God had been preparing Philomena for this mission, cultivating within her a particular devotion to the Sacred Heart of Jesus, Mary Immaculate, and Saint Michael: "This new Trinity must be blessed and glorified on earth, as is the Unity of the Three Divine Persons in Heaven. Happy the nation, happy the country or the monastery which shall be fired with this devotion. Write all thou knowest of it."

In a letter to her confessor Philomena wrote:

> It may be said that between Jesus, Mary, and the Archangel Michael there is but one will, but one desire. Oh, a thousand times happy are those devoted to them, devoted

> to the most Holy Heart of Jesus, or more, to that of his Immaculate Mother, or still more, to the Seraphic Archangel Saint Michael; for, as I have remarked, the glory that each one of them receives from this devotion will be equally shared by the two others.

Philomena added, "Mary wills to ask, Jesus or his Most Sacred Heart wills to grant, and Saint Michael wills to distribute generously what Mary has obtained."

How, then, did Philomena make known the greatness of Saint Michael, as he commanded? Philomena oriented her life around prayer: using mortifications (wearing a hair shirt and self-flagellation) in the early hours of the morning; practicing continual prayer from three until six in the afternoon modeled on Jesus in the Garden of Gethsemane; praying the Divine Office with her fellow sisters; participating in Holy Mass; and fasting three days a week on bread and water, among other such penances. Philomena's order, the barefooted Minims, a contemplative order founded by Saint Francis of Paola in the 1400s, already practiced a severe diet, such as excluding meat at all times. In the last year of her life, Philomena fasted all but one day during the month of May, eating just a piece of bread, sustained only by holy Communion the rest of the month.

Yet such physical sufferings revealed a joy she credited to her "Trinity," which she hoped her order would propagate beyond the cloister: "the worship of the New Trinity, the Very Sweet Heart of Jesus, His Mother, the Immaculate Virgin Mary, and the Archangel Michael."

Only twenty-three years after her death, Pope Leo XIII proclaimed Philomena "Venerable," recognizing her as a model of virtue and sanctity.

Pope Pius IX

When Italian troops entered Rome in 1870, the unification of Italy, a process known as *Risorgimento*, was complete. The Kingdom of Italy, with its capital in Turin, was ruled by the powerful House of Savoy (who would continue to rule until the abdication of King Umberto II and establishment of a republic in 1946). Also in 1870, the last monarchical ruler of France, Napoleon III, capitulated his emperorship in the Franco-Prussian War. The Third Republic succeeded the monarchy, intent on modernizing France. To the National Assembly, modernization meant an anticlerical attitude toward the Church and its venerable legacy, from its glorious cathedrals to towns and villages that had quietly absorbed the Faith since the time of Clovis. Much of this seismic change occurred during the pontificate of Pope Pius IX (1846–1878), the longest reigning pontiff in the Roman Catholic Church, aside from Saint Peter.

Born Giovanni Maria Mastai-Ferretti in 1792 at Senigallia off the Adriatic coast in the Papal States, Giovanni was the youngest of nine. At age eleven, after a period of homeschooling, Giovanni attended St. Michael's School in Tuscany. His sovereign ruler in the Papal States, Pope Pius VII, was embattled by aggression from Napoleon, and it was young Giovanni's dream to serve his pontiff not as a priest but as a member of the Papal Noble Guard, a group similar to the Swiss Guards.[2]

Epilepsy forced Giovanni to return home from St. Michael's School after six years, as well as to surrender his hope of joining the Papal Noble Guard. With a dispensation from Pius VII regarding his epilepsy, Giovanni became a priest in 1819. Shortly after his ordination, following his participation in a Vatican delegation to Chile and Peru, Father Giovanni was appointed director of the Hospice of San Michele in Rome. Giovanni became Pius IX in 1846.

During his reign, the pervading new world order reshaped the heart and soul of Christendom. Directly affected by this was a most hallowed site: Mont-Saint-Michel. By the second half of the nineteenth century, Mont-Saint-Michel was already a ghost of its former spiritual self: the few remaining monks had long been removed and the ancient monastery closed in 1790. The monastery became a prison, an Alcatraz-type location that authorities found suitable for dissidents of the French Revolution. Most of these prisoners were Catholic clerics.

Champions of Mont-Saint-Michel's unique stature as a religious nexus, like Victor Hugo — also deeply responsible for preserving Notre-Dame's prominence in Paris through his *The Hunchback of Notre-Dame* — influenced Third Republic policy enough that Mont-Saint-Michel was listed as an historic monument in 1874. Yet it was not until after World War I in the following century that worship was allowed to resume on the mount.

But signs of France's true Catholic soul, such as rallying behind Mont-Saint-Michel and Notre-Dame, continued to reveal its presence. During the modernization and reconstruction of Paris in the mid-1850s, city planners agreed a fountain and statue was to be erected at the opening of a huge new boulevard on the other side of the Seine from Notre-Dame. The statue was originally to be of Peace, a feminine goddess with echoes of the Revolution's Cult of Reason. With Napoleon III still in power at the time, a statue of Napoleon Bonaparte was also proposed, but rejected. What was agreed upon, finally, was a triumphal statue of Saint Michael trampling the devil. The corresponding boulevard, then, was named Boulevard Saint-Michel, and the bridge across the Seine, Pont-Saint-Michel. The statue remains an iconic Parisian landmark to this day.

Stripping the distinct religious nature of Mont-Saint-Michel during the French Revolution actually enhanced public devotion during the nineteenth century. Even amid secularization, Mont-Saint-Michel proved the French still longed for things of the spiritual realm. A silver statue of Saint Michael was crowned at the monastery by the authorization of Pope Pius IX on July 3, 1877. The thousands in attendance reaffirmed not only France's spiritual longing, but also how much devotion to Saint Michael had endured over the centuries. The crowning ceremony and the splendor of the place's Catholicity shook the anticlerical position of the Third Republic. The aggressive secular push in culture and politics could not accomplish the complete eradication of the Faith. The battle lines had been drawn: the God of Jesus Christ, his holy angels, saints, and his Mother were an inconvenient truth. Something Satan knew all along.

The stage was thus set for the October 13, 1884, vision of Pope Leo XIII.

A Prolific Pope

Gioacchino Pecci was born in 1810 just south of Siena. The young Pecci was educated by the Jesuits, shortly after Pope Pius VII lifted the suppression against the order that had been enforced since 1773. Pecci excelled in classics, theology, canon, and civil law — all before entering the priesthood. Finally, Pecci was ordained in 1837. As a nuncio and later as Bishop of Perugia, Pecci developed strong foreign relationships and was acutely aware of the civil and domestic issues everyday Catholics faced. Shortly before Pope Pius IX's death, Pecci was appointed *camerlengo* in August 1877, the chief Vatican administrator who oversees the functions of the Holy See at the time of a pope's death. Six months later, Cardinal Pecci succeeded Pius as Pope Leo XIII.

Having devoted forty years to priestly life in the field, Pope Leo XIII was equipped with the awareness of the Church's challenges and the various ways in which Satan and his minions were working in the world. Within two months of his election, Pope Leo produced his first encyclical, *Inscrutabili Dei Consilio* (On the Evils of Society). Eighty-six more encyclicals followed over the next twenty-four and a half years. Three encyclicals alone were produced in the first half of 1884, the first on France, the second on freemasonry, and the third on the rosary. Clearly, this was a pope up to the task of defending the Faith in a time hostile to it. He thought, prayed, and worked as if the Lord might call him home at any day. When he finally breathed his last at the age of ninety-three on July 20, 1903, the legacy of Pope Leo XIII had long been cemented.

And yet for as prolific a pope as he was, perhaps Leo XIII may be best remembered for the simple, fearless prayer he composed on a Monday in October 1884.

The Vision of Pope Leo XIII

Father Domenic Pehenino describes an unusual spiritual experience of Pope Leo XIII on October 13, 1884.[3] "One morning the great Pope Leo XIII had celebrated a Mass and, as usual, was attending a Mass of thanksgiving. Suddenly, we saw him raise his head and stare at something above the celebrant's head. He was staring motionlessly, without batting an eye. His expression was one of horror and awe; the color and look on his face changing rapidly. Something unusual and grave was happening in him." Other accounts assert the pope was the principal celebrant in his private chapel in the Vatican when the incident occurred. In any event, Pope Leo XIII, six years into his pontificate and at the age of seventy-four, fell into trancelike state at the foot of the altar, frozen, unmoving, his face terrified. Aides feared he was suffering some kind of paralytic seizure, not unlike those experienced by Pius IX throughout his life.

Ten minutes later Leo recovered, but was no more relaxed. It was as if something was bottled inside him and he needed to expunge it. What resulted that day was the composition of the Prayer to Saint Michael, a much-needed exhortation from the Vicar of Christ himself, an almost personal appeal from the Successor of Saint Peter on behalf of his global flock:

> Saint Michael, the Archangel, defend us in battle, be our protection against the wickedness and snares of the devil; may God rebuke him, we humbly pray; and do thou, O Prince of the heavenly host, by the power of God, thrust into hell Satan and all the evil spirits who wander through the world for the ruin of souls. Amen.

The invocation was given such importance it was among the rare nonliturgical elements added to the Mass, included as part of the Leonine Prayers recited at the foot of the altar. Catholics around the world recited the prayer after Mass until the 1960s. According to a 1946 Pastoral Letter to the Diocese of Bologna, Cardinal Nasalli Rocca wrote, "[Pope Leo XIII] would recite that prayer with strong, powerful voice: we heard it many a time in the Vatican Basilica."[4]

But what transfixed Leo at the foot of the altar? A popular story around this time described the Pope hearing two voices, one guttural and one gentle, emanate from the tabernacle area, which he deemed to be one of Satan, and one of Our Lord.

> The guttural voice, the voice of Satan, boasting: "I can destroy your Church."
> The gentle voice of Our Lord: "You can? Then go ahead and do so."
> Satan: "To do so, I need more time and more power."
> Our Lord: "How much time? How much power?"
> Satan: "Seventy-five to one hundred years, and a greater power over those who will give themselves over to my service."
> Our Lord: "You have the time, you will have the power. Do with them what you will."[5]

While it may be interesting to try to calculate the timeframe granted to Satan for his feckless goal or to debate the authenticity of the exchange, Leo XIII's immense contribution to spiritual combat resulted in an explosive resurgence in devotion to Saint Michael — just as a secular rebellion, a questioning of things divine, began to take shape. Leo's private secretary, Monsignor Rinaldo Angeli, later claimed Leo foresaw demonic forces descending upon Rome in another supernatural encounter. Cardinal Rocca continued in his pastoral letter, "Leo XIII also personally wrote an exorcism that is included in the Roman Ritual [1954 edition, XII, C. III, p. 863 and following]. He recommended that bishops and priests read these exorcisms often in their dioceses and parishes. He himself would recite them often throughout the day."[6]

The Chaplet of Saint Michael

The history of the chaplet derives from a tradition regarding a Portuguese Carmelite nun, Antónia d'Astónaco, who experienced a private revelation sometime in the 1750s. In her revelation, Saint Michael appeared and provided Sister Antónia the formula for praying the chaplet, which includes nine salutations for each of the choir of angels (see Appendix A). Saint Michael promised that whoever would practice this devotion in his honor would have, when approaching holy Communion, an escort of nine angels chosen from each of the nine choirs. In addition, to those who would recite the chaplet daily, he promised his continual assistance and that of all the holy angels during life, and after death deliverance from purgatory for themselves and their relations.

Details of the life of Sister Antónia d'Astónaco are scant, yet she is a Servant of God, meaning her cause for sainthood has been formally opened. In 1851, Pope Pius IX approved the use of the Chaplet of St. Michael with the following indulgences: "a hundred days for every day on which the chaplet is worn or the medal of angels attached to it is kissed, seven years and quarantines for each recital, and for daily recital a plenary every month and on four feast-days in that year."[7] A year before his death, Pius IX insisted those priests capable of blessing objects must include the Chaplet of St. Michael.

The Scapular of Saint Michael

In 1878, a confraternity named after Saint Michael was founded at Sant'Eustachio in Rome, and promoted the scapular of Saint Michael. Shortly before he died, Pope Pius IX gave his blessing for the use of the scapular. When Pope Leo XIII succeeded Pius IX, the new pope not only granted the specific indulgences to the confraternity, but also formally approved the use of the scapular associated with it. Two years later, Leo XIII elevated the confraternity as the Archconfraternity of the Scapular of Saint Michael.[8]

The Congregation of Rites approved the formula for blessing and investing with the scapular in 1883, here translated into English:

V. Our help is in the name of the Lord.

R. Who made heaven and earth.

V. The Lord be with you.
R. And with thy spirit.

Let us pray. O Almighty, everlasting God, Who dost graciously defend thy Church from the wiles of the devil through Saint Michael the Archangel, we suppliantly implore thee to bless † and sanctify † this token introduced for arousing and fostering devotion among thy faithful toward this great protector. And do thou grant all who wear it may be strengthened by the same holy archangel, so as to vanquish the enemies of body and soul, both in this life and at the hour of death. Through Christ our Lord.
R. Amen

The priest then sprinkles the scapular with holy water, and bestows it, saying:

Receive brother (sister), the scapular of Saint Michael the Archangel, so that by his constant intercession thou mayest be disposed to lead a holy life.
R. Amen.

Let us pray. We appeal to thy goodness, O Lord that thou wouldst hear our prayers and graciously bless † this servant (handmaid) of thine, who has been placed under the special patronage of Saint Michael the Archangel. Through his intercession may he (she) avoid and guard against whatever is displeasing to thee, and thus merit in serving thee to accomplish his (her) own sanctification and that of others. Through Christ our Lord. Amen.[9]

The Catholic Encyclopedia describes the scapular as having "the form of a small shield; of these one is made of blue and the other of black cloth, and of the bands likewise one is blue and the other black. Both portions of the scapular bear the well-known representation of the Archangel Saint Michael slaying the dragon, and the inscription '*Quis ut Deus*.'"

The wave of devotion as chronicled in this chapter bolstered the faithful's ardor for Saint Michael during a time of unparalleled technological and industrial expansion. These spiritual tools remain available for those seeking to remain fixed on God during our arduous earthly journey.

7

Angel of Peace

While images of Michael invoke war and combat, his presence reflects the peace of God. We have seen how he remains a steadfast intercessor despite whatever tribulation threatens to overwhelm the life of faith at any given time.

One such trial occurred in 1631, one hundred years after the appearance of the Virgin of Guadalupe, when a plague was devastating Mexico. In the village of San Bernabe in the small state of Tlaxcala, east of Mexico City, the Greater Litanies procession was held on April 25. Tlaxcala had long been a site of heightened spirituality. Originally occupied by the ancient Olmecs, Tlaxcala was where the first cathedral was constructed in Mexico. And just as the Black Death ravaged Rome in 590, in 1631, smallpox plagued the municipality of Nativitas. Among those who suffered from the disease was a seventeen-year-old boy, Diego Lázaro. Nevertheless,

Diego participated in the solemn procession. And just as on April 25, 590, in the midst of the procession in Rome, Saint Michael appeared, but only to Diego Lázaro. In the apparition, Michael gave Diego directions to where a spring of water will cure those affected by smallpox.

Yet Diego Lázaro chose to ignore the encounter. His condition worsened, and he was anointed and given the last rites. At that moment Michael appeared again, transporting Diego to the location of the miraculous spring. Diego recounted the remarkable imagery:

> Saint Michael transported me to the place he had told me about before. With Saint Michael going before me through the night, everything was illuminated as the great prince passed, as if it were midday. Rocks and branches split apart as he passed, clearing a path for us. As we reached a certain spot, I saw Saint Michael holding a golden staff topped with a cross.
>
> "From the place I touch with this staff you will see flowing the miraculous spring I told you about during the procession. Make it clear to everyone that the illness you have suffered is a fruit of your disobedience."
>
> Having said this, there was suddenly a great whirlwind of deafening screams, wailing and moaning, as if a great crowd were being driven from the place. I shook with fear. It seemed to me that the entire mountain ridge would tumble down on top of me during the turmoil.
>
> "Do not fear; these are the sounds made by the demons, thine enemies, because they know the great benefits that through my intercession the faithful will receive in this place from Our Lord. Many, seeing the marvels worked here, will convert and do penance for their sins, and all will give thanks to God for his mercies. Those who approach this spring with lively faith and sorrow for their faults will, with the water from this spring, obtain relief in their sufferings and needs, and those at the point of death

will find a comfort in these waters."

Having said this, I then saw a brilliant light descent from heaven, piercing the ground at the site of the spring. Saint Michael continued,

"This light that you have seen descend from heaven is the virtue that God in his Divine Providence gives in this spring for the health and relief of the sick and needy. Make this known at once to everyone. That they may believe your testimony, I promise to work a great prodigy through you."

With that, Saint Michael disappeared, and I found myself here in this hut once again, completely cured.[1]

The date of this second apparition to Diego Lázaro was May 8, 1631, the same date as the apparition of Saint Michael at Monte Gargano. The spring was soon publicly discovered, and three official investigations concluded Diego was not fabricating the story. Health returned to the inhabitants of the region, and the spring was named Saint Michael's Well. Today, the area in Nativitas where Diego Lázaro brought hope to his afflicted people is known as San Miguel del Milagro — the Miracle of Saint Michael.

Though Saint Michael is undeniably associated with themes of spiritual combat and warfare, his service to the Trinity makes him an icon of peace. As related in the story of Diego Lázaro, this angel of peace calms the soul in times of great cultural crises.

The Great War

On July 13, 1917, an apparition of the Blessed Virgin Mary revealed three "secrets" to three children at the Cova da Iria fields outside Aljustrel, near the village of Fátima, in Portugal. The eldest child and longest survivor of the Fátima seers, Sister Lucia produced numerous memoirs prior to her death in 2005. This third secret was put to paper in 1944 by order of the Bishop of Leiria, Fátima's regional bishop. Sister Lucia begins:

> After the two parts which I have already explained, at the left of Our Lady and a little above, we saw an Angel with a flaming sword in his left hand; flashing, it gave out flames that looked as though they would set the world on fire; but they died out in contact with the splendor that Our Lady radiated towards him from her right hand: pointing to the earth with his right hand, the Angel cried out in a loud voice: 'Penance, Penance, Penance!'[2]

The identity of the angel with the flaming sword is not stated. Cardinal Joseph Ratzinger, the future Pope Benedict XVI, postulated in his theological commentary on the secret, "The angel with the flaming sword on the left of the Mother of God recalls similar images in the Book of Revelation. This represents the threat of judgment which looms over the world. Today the prospect that the world might be reduced to ashes by a sea of fire no longer seems pure fantasy: man himself, with his inventions, has forged the flaming sword."[3]

The July 13, 1917, vision was one in a number of monthly experiences the three children encountered at the Cova da Iria, culminating in the famous "Miracle of the Sun" witnessed by seventy thousand people on October 13, 1917 — thirty-three years to the date of Leo XIII's vision that inspired the Prayer to Saint Michael. The phenomena at Fátima was a welcomed burst of light amid the fog of war. For this was the time of the Great War, World War I (1914–1918), the cataclysmic conflict that besieged and afflicted countries that only a century before shrugged off their heritage and declared themselves liberated from the arcane governance of monarchies. In a way, the war was a bloody result of the political upheavals which we examined to some degree in previous chapters. The war's western front, for instance, hauntingly evoked the past of both France and Christendom with places such as Reims, the coronation site of kings, under assault and in many ways forever changed. These locales were also the battlegrounds for the Hundred Years' War, when Catholic brethren fought each other, just as

St. Michael Vanquishing the Angel, 1518 / Raphael, Manuel Arbós y Ayerbe / Public domain

they were doing in the twentieth century. On May 23, 1915, Italy officially entered World War I by declaring war on Austria-Hungary. The following day, the Austro-Hungarians responded with a naval bombardment targeting, among other locations, the rail station in Manfredonia — in the shadow of Michael's beloved grotto of Monte Gargano.

Among the sixty million soldiers who fought in World War I was a sickly Capuchin in the Italian Medical Corps, Private Francesco Forgione. Born in 1887 in Pietrelcina, Italy, the young man was ordained a priest in 1910. Drafted at the outset of the war in 1914, medical issues forced Private Forgione out of service for a time before returning in 1917. A few months after his permanent discharge in March 1918, this Capuchin friar began to experience the highly unusual and mystical experience of the stigmata. Based at Our Lady of Grace Capuchin Friary in the Gargano Mountains, near the Sanctuary of Monte Sant'Angelo, the friar would not only often visit the grotto dedicated to Saint Michael but would also send penitents there as well. This veteran of the Great War who died in 1968 was better known throughout the world as Padre Pio.

World War II

During World War II (1939–1945), Saint Michael earned the title of patron for paratroopers, namely the 82nd Airborne Division, the infantry division of the United States Army whose deployment from the sky dramatically helped secure Allied victory. The images of brave troops ominously descending to earth were not unlike the fallen angels cast out of heaven. Only this time, these members of the Greatest Generation fought on the side of good. The soldiers were arriving to quash one of the most dangerous manifestations of mass evil the world had ever seen.

Guy LoFaro, 82nd Airborne Division combat veteran and former professor of history at West Point, authored a sprawling account of the 82nd Airborne Division entitled *The Sword of St. Michael.*[4] Little known to civilians, the airborne division's devotion to Saint Michael continues and is celebrated annually with what is dubbed the St. Michael's Day Jump. A venerable 82nd Airborne Division tradition, the event emphasizes not only the division's attachment to Saint Michael, but also the spiritual component of their role as paratroopers. Chaplains instruct the paratroopers on the historicity of the day's jump, and educate the troops on the role of Saint Michael himself throughout history. Colonel Randy Griffin, 82nd Airborne Division chaplain, commented in an article published by the U.S. Army, "The St. Michael's Jump and the recognition of Saint Michael as the archangel that watches over and protects paratroopers, that understanding, that concept, has been around since the conception of the airborne community."[5]

The date of St. Michael's Day Jump is none other than May 8.

Saint Michael's reach, therefore, evangelizes past the bounds of one's religious identity, physical borders, and time. Just as Michael burst through the heavenly realm to inspire those here on earth, just as he was venerated in both Judaism and Christianity, in the East and West, by multiple nations and peoples, Michael's duty to safeguard knows no bounds. In this way, as heavenly protector, Saint Michael — in addition to his patronage of military personnel, paramedics, mariners, grocers, and doctors — is also the patron of police officers. An old, anonymous "Policeman's Prayer to Saint Michael" reads as follows:

> Saint Michael, Heaven's glorious Commissioner of Police, who once so neatly and successfully cleared God's premises of all undesirables, look with a kindly and professional eye on your earthly force. Give us cool heads, stout hearts, hard punches, an uncanny flair for investigation, and wise judgment. Make us the terror of burglars, the friend of children and law-abiding citizens, kind to strangers, polite to bores, strict with law-breakers, and impervious to temptations. You know, Saint Michael, from your own experiences with the devil, that the policeman's lot on earth is not always a happy one; but your sense of duty that so pleased God, your hard knocks that so surprised the dev-

il, and your angelic self-control give us inspiration. And when we lay down our night sticks, enroll us in your heavenly force, where we will be as proud to guard the throne of God, as we have been to guard the city of men. Amen.

8
Saint Michael and the Mass

Michael's tireless loyalty to the Incarnate Word in heaven is rewarded by his exalted position among the holy angels. The intimate relationship between Michael and the Son of God is fulfilled in the Passion of Christ on earth, in the Jerusalem under Roman occupation in the first century. The Resurrection, Ascension, and moments of the Acts of the Apostles also detail angelic involvement, and the work of Michael and the angels does not conclude with the New Testament. Specifically, Michael's relationship to Christ is best indicated by Michael's exalted place in the Sacred Liturgy, the holiest prayer, where Christ continually gives himself, Body and Blood, Soul and Divinity, as nourishment for the salvation of souls.

Altarpiece of St Michael (central panel) c. 1510 / Gerard David, Public domain

Michael and Holy Mass

A nineteenth-century English priest, Frederick William Faber, suggested Michael is present not only during Mass, but especially during its highest point, the Eucharist. "It is said that Saint Michael revealed to Saint Eutropius the Hermit that he had been chosen to be the guardian angel of the Blessed Sacrament," Father Faber noted, "and that it had been entrusted to his charge ever since Holy Thursday."[1]

In the Roman calendar revised by Pope Saint Paul VI in 1970, Michael's feast day is celebrated with fellow archangels Gabriel and Raphael on September 29. The prayers for the day include invocations to all the archangels, but the second reading of the Mass specifically details Michael's battle with the devil from Revelation 12. Increasingly, more parishes also incorporate Pope Leo XIII's Prayer to Saint Michael recited at the foot of the altar following the conclusion of Mass. Such a verbal invocation strengthens the communal bond of not only devotion to Saint Michael, but also a concerted effort to avoid evil.

For many centuries, September 29 was devoted solely to Michael himself. Known as Michaelmas Day, it was considered so major a feast — especially in pre-Reformation England and Ireland — that it was sanctioned a Holy Day of Obligation until the seventeenth century.

The 1962 Roman Missal contains the beautiful Propers on Michaelmas Day, here translated in English:

Collect

O God, who wondrously directs the services of angels and men, grant that our lives on earth may be guarded by the angels who stand ever before your face ministering to you in heaven. Through Our Lord …

Alleluia

Alleluia, alleluia!

Holy archangel Michael, defend us in battle, that we may not perish in the dreaded judgment. Alleluia!

Postcommunion

We rely on the prayers of the blessed archangel Michael, O Lord, that the Sacrament which we have received upon our lips may always remain in our hearts. Through Our Lord …

In the Confiteor of the Extraordinary Form, Michael is among the elect implored by the faithful. One confesses sorrow and reparation for sins, seeking forgiveness of venial sins, and forgiveness before not only God, but also the Blessed Virgin Mary, and the angels and saints, including Michael the Archangel. Michael is invoked once again at the offertory during a high Mass. After offering the sacrifice of bread, wine, and all the faithful, the priest blesses the incense, saying: "By the intercession of blessed Michael the Archangel, who standeth at the right hand of the altar of incense, and of all his elect, may the Lord deign to bless this incense, and to accept its fragrant sweetness. Through Christ our Lord. Amen."

After the priest incenses the altar, the server then incenses the gathered, including the faithful in this solemn act of offertory. Here, the prayers of Michael and all the holy ones are invoked, as in the Confiteor, uniting penitent with the sacrifice. It also recalls the image from Revelation: "The smoke of the incense rose with the prayers of the saints from the hand of the angel before God" (Rv 8:4). This is not a mere gesture of piety, but encompasses Michael's prime roles and mission as guardian, protector, and messenger. Catholic art has frequently depicted the invisible multitude of angels, saints, and blessed gathered, if not hovering, around the altar in eager anticipation to join the faithful in prayer and thanksgiving, particularly at the consecration.

At the offertory in a Requiem Mass for the dead, Saint Michael is specifically mentioned:

> O Lord Jesus Christ, King of glory, deliver the souls of all the faithful departed from the pains of hell and from the bottomless pit: deliver them from the lion's mouth, that hell swallow them not up, that they fall not into darkness, but let the standard-bearer, holy Michael, lead them into that holy light; which Thou didst promise of old to Abraham and to his seed.
>
> *V.* We offer to Thee, O Lord, sacrifices and prayers: do Thou receive them in behalf of those souls of whom we make memorial this day. Grant them, O Lord, to pass from death to that life which Thou didst promise of old to Abraham and to his seed.

Saint Michael and the Byzantine Divine Liturgy

Michael is celebrated in the Byzantine Catholic Church on November 8, formally known as the Synaxis (Assembly) of the Chief of the Heavenly Hosts, Archangel Michael, and the Other Heavenly Bodiless Powers.[2] November 8 is a date deliberately chosen to honor these celestial beings. In the ancient Greek calendar, March was the first month of the year, making November the ninth month. Thus a feast day was established in November, since there are nine choirs of angels. "The eighth day of the month was chosen for the Synaxis of all the Bodiless Powers of Heaven since the Day of the Dread Last Judgment is called the Eighth Day by the holy Fathers. After the end of this age (characterized by its seven days of Creation) will come the Eighth Day, and then 'the Son of Man shall come in His Glory and all the holy Angels with Him' (Mt 25:31)."[3]

The troparion (a short hymn or stanza) for the Divine Liturgy on November 8 petitions:

> Commanders of the heavenly hosts,
> we who are unworthy beseech you,
> by your prayers encompass us beneath the wings of your immaterial glory,
> and faithfully preserve us who fall down and cry to you:
> "Deliver us from all harm, for you are the commanders of the powers on high!"[4]

The kontakion for November 8 reads:

> Commanders of God's armies and ministers of the divine glory,
> princes of the bodiless angels and guides of mankind,
> ask for what is good for us, and for great mercy,
> supreme commanders of the bodiless hosts.[5]

The concluding chant of the Akathist Hymn for Saint Michael, a lengthy, detailed hymn dedicated to a specific saint or event, implores:

> Archangel Michael, we are attacked day and night by the evil enemy of God, by that arrogant liar and vile destroyer of souls, by that serpent which through falsehood and foolishness desires to rob the Holy Church of her faithful. We come to you, O leader of the archangels and angels, in our need for defense against unbelief and for enlightenment over doubt. Grant us shelter beneath your strong and glorious wings, that we may discern and overcome all temptations and attacks. Help us to live in fidelity to our mother the Church and to Our Father in heaven. Amen.[6]

Through this study of Michael's involvement in the liturgy, we are invited to draw deeper into the mystery of the Holy Sacrifice of the Mass. Invoking Michael's intercession brings us closer to the Church Triumphant during the celebration of the liturgy. We can ask Michael to bring our prayers and petitions before the Father, and in doing so develop a deeper devotion to the Holy Eucharist.

View of St. Michael reredos below the all-seeing-eye-of-God at Mission San Miguel in San Miguel, California / James Day

9
Saint Michael and Death

In Jewish eschatology, Michael is the guide of souls in death; he is the one who will sound the trumpet for the dead to rise.[1] This belief continues into Christian tradition. As through one's life, Saint Michael's role at the hour of death is also associated with safeguarding and protection. These last moments of earthly life offer one final opportunity for Satan to unleash an attack — the last chance to bring souls to the netherworld.

"With regard to the assaults of Satan, know that the all-just God permits him to have great power to assail us at the hour of death; not indeed for our perdition, but for our probation," wrote a seventeenth-century German priest, Father Martin von Cochem, OSFC. Father Cochem continued:

> Before expiring the Christian has yet to prove that nothing can avail to make him forsake his God. For this reason

> the evil enemy employs all the power he has received, and brings all his forces to bear upon a man when he is dying, in the hope of casting him to sin, and thrusting him down to hell. During our whole lifetime he attacks us fiercely, and neglects no means whereby he may deceives us. But all these persecutions do not bear comparison with the final onslaught with which he endeavors to overcome us at the last. Then he raves and rages, like a roaring lion, seeking whom he may devour.[2]

The Church urges recitation of the Hail Mary, invocation to Saint Michael, and prayers to Saint Joseph for a happy and holy death. Here in this trinity of saints, the dying are entrusted as penitents brought before the merciful love of the Triune God. In the 1962 "Rite for Commending a Departing Soul," the priest prays over the dying: "Let him (her) be welcomed by Saint Michael, the archangel of God, who has won the leadership of the heavenly host." The Extraordinary Form Mass for the Dead prayer at the offertory also implores, "May the standard bearer, Saint Michael, lead them into the holy light."

Numerous saints detail in their spiritual writings Saint Michael's presence at death. Saint Alphonsus Liguori (1696–1787) details an anecdote of a deathbed conversion by the intercession of Saint Michael:

> A certain Polish gentleman had for many years led a wicked life. When the hour of death approached, he was filled with terror and tortured by remorse of conscience over his former recklessness, so that he was reduced to a state of utter despair. No amount of exhortation or encouragement had any effect upon him; he refused every spiritual consolation.
>
> This unhappy man, however, still had some veneration for Saint Michael, and God in his mercy permitted the holy archangel to appear to him in his last struggle.

> Saint Michael encouraged him to repentance and said that he had prayed and obtained for him sufficient time to regulate the affairs of his soul. Shortly afterwards, two Dominican priests came to the house, saying that a stranger had sent them. The sick man recognized this as the work of Saint Michael. He confessed his sins amid tears of repentance, received Holy Communion with touching devotion, and breathed forth his soul with every indication of being truly reconciled with God.

Saint Alphonsus and other saints have also expounded on Saint Michael as the guardian of purgatory, one who will remain in his role as protector of souls as the righteous are purified to meet the eternal light of the Holy Face.

Scales of Souls

Michael's tempered use of the sword — that is, justice, depicted in sacred art by the holding of scales — illustrates wisdom and understanding, let alone fortitude. Michael's exemplary display of fortitude is echoed by American author Henry Adams on his study of Mont-Saint-Michel: "He is the conqueror of Satan, the mightiest of all created spirits, the nearest to God. His place was where the danger was greatest."[3]

Saint Louis de Montfort (1673–1716) utilized the image of the scales in relation to a soul's sins. In his *Secret of the Rosary*, de Montfort — whose devotion of total consecration to Jesus through Mary has developed a large following in modern times — relates an anecdote regarding "a certain pious but self-willed lady from Rome." He writes:

> Later on, when she was at prayer she fell into ecstasy and had a vision of her soul appearing before the Supreme Judge. Saint Michael put all her penances and other prayers on one side of the scales and all her sins and imperfections on the other. The tray of her good works was

greatly outweighed by that of her sins and imperfections.

Saint Louis also relates an apocryphal tale about Saint Mary Magdalene:

> Few saints have reached the same heights of prayer as Saint Mary Magdalene, who was lifted up to heaven by angels each day, and who had the privilege of learning at the feet of Jesus and his holy Mother. Yet one day, when she asked God to show her a sure way of advancing in his love and arriving at the heights of perfection, he sent the archangel Saint Michael to tell her, on his behalf, that there was no other way for her to reach perfection than to meditate on Our Lord's Passion. So he placed a cross in the front of her cave and told her to pray before it, contemplating the sorrowful mysteries which she had seen take place with her own eyes.

Last, Saint Louis de Montfort urges daily recitation of the Most Holy Rosary. It should come as no surprise that the saying of the Rosary typically ends with the prayer to Saint Michael.

The End Times

"But you, Daniel, shut up the words, and seal the book, until the end of time. Many shall run back and forth, and knowledge shall increase," the Prophet Daniel is told in chapter 12 of the Book of Daniel (12:4). What is this message Daniel is told to keep secret? As we read earlier,

> At that time shall arise Michael, the great prince who has charge of your people. And there shall be a time of trouble, such as never has been since there was a nation till that time; but at that time your people shall be delivered, every one whose name shall be found written in the book. And many of those who sleep in the dust of the earth shall

> awake, some to everlasting lie, and some to shame and everlasting contempt. And those who are wise shall shine like the brightness of the firmament; and those who turn many to righteousness like the stars for ever and ever. (Dn 12:1–3)

So opens the Book of Daniel; as in the first great battle, so too will Michael return at the end for the final confrontation. The history of the Church and specifically the *Catechism* speaks of this final battle, not for sensationalist purposes, but in order to prepare the soul:

> Before Christ's second coming the Church must pass through a final trial that will shake the faith of many believers. The persecution that accompanies her pilgrimage on earth will unveil the "mystery of iniquity" in the form of a religious deception offering men an apparent solution to their problems at the price of apostasy from the Truth. The supreme religious deception is that of the Antichrist, a pseudo-messianism by which man glorifies himself in the place of God and of his Messiah come in the flesh. (CCC 675)

In 1976, Cardinal Karol Wojtyla stated the following during a tour of the United States:

> We are now standing in the face of the greatest historical confrontation humanity has gone through. I do not think that wide circles of American society or wide circles of the Christian community realize this fully. We are now facing the final confrontation between the Church and the anti-Church, of the Gospel versus the anti-Gospel. ...
>
> We must be prepared to undergo great trials in the not-too-distant future; trials that will require us to be ready to give up even our lives, and a total gift of self to

> Christ and for Christ. Through your prayers and mine, it is possible to alleviate this tribulation, but it is no longer possible to avert it. ... How many times has the renewal of the Church been brought about in blood! It will not be different this time.[4]

Our entire journey with Saint Michael, throughout Scripture in both the Old and New Testament, from Church history and tradition, to the Sacraments, the Most Holy Eucharist and the Holy Sacrifice of the Mass — and in the works of the brave and fearless who found a model of courage in Saint Michael — all of it leads toward the end, both of one's time on earth, and even that of the Church, which as the *Catechism* reminds us, is only here as a pilgrim on earth.

10
Saint Michael and You

"Who is that, Mom?" I once asked, gazing at the angel in the stained-glass window, when I could finally articulate what had been long steeped in my childhood consciousness.

"That's who our church is named after," my mother replied quietly. "That's Saint Michael."

Saint Michael is more than just the patron saint of my childhood parish and school. Through his presence in Scripture and Tradition, the liturgy, secular and church history, art and architecture, and his impact on the lives of popes and saints, Saint Michael has emerged as a powerful intercessor for guidance and protection, taking our prayers and petitions to the merciful throne of Almighty God. We can be sure of this especially when we are struggling in the heat of spiritual battle, surrounded by temptations and the snares of the devil.

St. Michael statue by Joseph Motto, c. 1956, St. Michael's Church, Independence, Ohio / Susan Synek

Saint Michael also challenges us. He challenges us by his very name, *Quis ut Deus?* — "who is like God?" Our modern age might suggest any number of options to answer that question. But it is a verse from the Psalmist which has the best response: "For who is God, but the LORD?" (Ps 18:31). We are challenged to overcome the allure of the worship of graven images and idols in place of God. Relativism excuses any kind of behavior under the banner of one's personal truth. In this way, one's ego may become one's god. While the Catholic Faith demands discipline, and the path to holiness is not an easy road, by its nature the Faith collects the three states of the church (Church Triumphant, Church Militant, and Church Penitent) to serve something greater than itself: the Blessed Trinity.

Saint Michael challenges us to better understand our faith's history. As we have seen, Michael's influence dates to the early centuries of Christianity; we have accounts of his intercessions, so many of which changed the destiny of entire nations. This history is our Catholic history. We are part of a rich tradition, and we yearn for Michael to once again bend our culture toward the light of faith. The Church has left a trove of spiritual fruits for every day and age anchored by the Eucharistic Lord waiting to be discovered, waiting to transform a world too often enclosed and resistant to the depth and breadth of God (cf. Eph 3:14).

Michael's fearlessness to confront evil is a challenge for us to cultivate an interior life and to discern spirits, to determine what is of God and what is not. Michael challenges us to better understand the Mass, to become more involved in contemplation of the Paschal Mystery, and wonder at the Incarnation. He challenges to reverence, to step out of ourselves, and in the silence of our daily prayer ask, "What do you want from me, God?"

We died with Christ in baptism, when our godparents on our behalf promised to reject Satan and all his works. This, then, uniquely attaches us to Saint Michael, whose mission remains to trample Satan, sword at the ready. Michael challenges us to live both a holy life and a holy death. "If God is with us," Pope Pius XII asked on February 11, 1949, "who is there that could overcome us?

In the final hour we shall stand victorious with Saint Michael, the Archangel, and share in the triumph of the Heavenly Jerusalem!"

Let us return for a final moment to Father Martin von Cochem's treatise on the Four Last Things. In his explication on the Final Judgment, Father Cochem references Saint Paul's Letter to the Romans: "We shall all stand before the judgment seat of God" (14:10). Father Cochem suggests Saint Michael will present the unrepentant before Christ, and Lucifer will accuse all of mankind to receive the same condemnation as he did when cast from Paradise. Father Cochem then postulates each will be led by their guardian angel to the judgment seat, with the enemy bringing forward every charge against them. The accused will be defended by his or her guardian angel, and set all good deeds on the scales of divine justice. "And if they are not too light, Christ will array him in the new robe, the garment of splendor, and crown him with the diadem of the eternal kingdom."[1] In the ensuing ascension of the good into everlasting glory, Father Cochem believes Saint Michael "will head the glorious procession, carrying the cross whereon Christ died."[2]

While such events remain to be seen, perhaps the Book of Sirach offers simple instruction on how to best prepare for the inevitable Four Last Things: "In whatever you do, remember your last days, and you will never sin" (7:36).

From the obscure depths of the ninth choir of angels, Michael dramatically triumphed in the War of Heaven to become God's fearless angel. It is in Michael's great moment of victory that he challenges us once more. Each and every day of our lives presents challenges of its own. We must actively promote the triumph of humility: to find sanctity in the rejected and to give hope to the forgotten and abandoned. In effect, to serve God as Michael did, so that "the last will be first, and the first last" (Mt 20:16).

ACKNOWLEDGMENTS

The genesis for this book began with an October 2018 article published in the *Orange County Catholic*, newspaper for the Diocese of Orange, on Saint Michael's role in a time of crisis. My thanks to the staff of Our Sunday Visitor, especially Mary Beth Giltner and Rebecca Martin, for their guidance and insight. I am forever indebted to my faith formation at Saint Michael's parish and school in Independence, Ohio, and the example of the Sisters of Notre Dame and Diocese of Cleveland priests. As always thanks to my wife, Christina, for her patience and support. By the time this book appears on bookshelves, our daughter Isla Rose Day will already be a few months old. Finally, my thanks to the late Jesuit philosopher Father James V. Schall, SJ, a prolific and prophetic writer and true priest. My brother, John, suggested writing something to honor Father Schall upon his death in April 2019, and so I dedicate this book to him.

APPENDIX A
Prayers

I. Prayers to Saint Michael

Prayer to St. Michael, the Archangel by Pope Leo XIII
Short Version
Saint Michael, the Archangel, defend us in battle, be our protection against the wickedness and snares of the devil; may God rebuke him, we humbly pray; and do thou, O Prince of the heavenly host, by the power of God, thrust into hell Satan and all evil spirits who wander through the world for the ruin of souls. Amen.

For Holy Church (Longer Version)
O glorious Prince of the heavenly host, Saint Michael, the Archangel, defend us in the battle and in the fearful warfare that we are waging against the principalities and powers, against the rulers of this world of darkness, against the evil spirits. Come thou, to the assistance of men, whom Almighty God created immortal, making them in his own image and likeness and redeeming them at a great price from the tyranny of Satan. Fight this day the battle of the Lord with thy legions of holy angels, even as of old, thou didst fight against Lucifer, the leader of the proud spirits and all his rebel Angels, who were powerless to stand against thee, neither was their place found anymore in heaven. And that apostle angel, transformed into an angel of darkness who still creeps about the earth to encompass our ruin, was cast headlong into the abyss together with his followers.

But, behold, that first enemy of mankind, and a murderer from the beginning, has regained his confidence. Changing himself into an angel of light, he goes about with the whole multitude of the wicked spirits to invade the earth and blot out the Name of God and of his Christ, to plunder, to slay, and to consign to eternal damnation the souls that have been destined for a crown of everlasting life. This wicked serpent, like an unclean torrent, pours into men of depraved minds and corrupt hearts the poison of his malice, the spirit of lying, impiety, and blasphemy, and the deadly breadth of impurity and every form of vice and iniquity. These crafty enemies of mankind have filled to overflowing with gall and wormwood the Church, which is the Bride of the Lamb without spot; they have laid profane hands upon her most sacred treasures.

Make haste, therefore, O invincible Prince, to help the people of God against the inroads of the lost spirits and grant us the victory. Amen.

Prayer for Protection of the Church and Her Members

O glorious Saint Michael, guardian and defender of the Church of Jesus Christ, come to the assistance of this Church, against which the powers of hell are unchained, guard with especial care her august head, and obtain that for him and for us the hour of triumph may speedily arrive. O glorious Archangel Saint Michael, watch over us during life, defend us against the assaults of the demon, assist us especially at the hour of death; obtain for us a favorable judgment, and the happiness of beholding God face to face for endless ages. Amen.

Invocation at the beginning of each Rosary

Saint Michael the Archangel,
With your light
Enlighten us.
With your wings
Protect us.
With your sword
Defend us.

Prayer to Saint Michael

Glorious Prince of the heavenly hosts and victor over rebellious spirits, be mindful of me who am so weak and sinful and yet so prone to pride and ambition. Lend me, I pray, thy powerful aid in every temptation and difficulty, and above all do not forsake me in my last struggle with the powers of evil. Amen.

Consecration of the Crown and the Kingdom to the Archangel

Prayer of Father Jean-Jacques Olier, founder of the Sulpicians

Glorious Saint Michael, Prince of the Heavenly Hosts and general of God's armies, I recognize you to be all powerful through Him over kingdoms and states. I submit myself to you with my entire court, my state, and my family, in order to live under your protection, and I renew myself as much as I am able, in the piety of all my predecessors who have always regarded you as their special protector. Thus, for the sake of the love that you have for this state, submit it entirely to God and to those who represent Him.

The Angelic Trisagion

Holy, Holy, Holy, Lord God of hosts, Heaven and earth are full of Thy glory.

Saint Michael, the Archangel, defend us in the battle, that we may not perish in the dreadful judgment.

For Help against Spiritual Enemies

Glorious Saint Michael, prince of the heavenly hosts, who stands always ready to give assistance the people of God; who fought with the dragon, the old serpent, and cast him out of heaven, and now valiantly defends the Church of God so the gates of hell may never prevail against her, I earnestly entreat you to assist me also in the painful and dangerous conflict which I sustain against the same formidable foe.

Be with me, O mighty Prince! that I may courageously fight and vanquish that proud spirit, whom thou, by the Divine power, gloriously overthrew, and whom our powerful King, Jesus Christ, in our nature, so completely overcome; so having triumphed over the enemy of my salvation, I may, with you and the holy angels, praise the clemency of God, who, though refusing mercy to the rebellious angels after their fall, has granted repentance and forgiveness to fallen man. Amen.

Consecration to Saint Michael

Saint Michael the Archangel, invincible prince of the angelic hosts and glorious protector of the universal Church, I greet thee and praise thee for that splendor with which God has adorned thee so richly. I thank God for the great graces he hast bestowed upon thee, especially to remain faithful when Lucifer and his followers rebelled, and to battle victoriously for the honor of God and the Divinity of the Son of Man.

Saint Michael, I consecrate to thee my soul and body. I choose thee as my patron and protector and entrust the salvation of my soul to thy care. Be the guardian of my obligation as a child of God and of the Catholic Church as again I renounce Satan, his works and pomps.

Assist me by thy powerful intercession in the fulfillment of these sacred promises, so that imitating thy courage and loyalty to God, and trusting in thy kind help and protection, I may be victorious over the enemies of my soul and be united with God in heaven forever. Amen.

Prayer for Perseverance

O God, thou hast made blessed Michael, thy archangel, victorious over the proud Lucifer and all the wicked spirits. We beseech thee that, combating under the cross and ever adopting his maxim, "Who is like unto God," we may be victorious over all our enemies, and be delivered from all evils. Regulate our lives according to thy will and commandments. Through Jesus Christ, Our Lord. Amen.

For Assistance at the Hour of Death
Glorious Archangel Saint Michael, by thy protection, enable my soul to be so enriched by grace as to be worthy to be presented by thee to Jesus Christ, my Judge, at the hour of my death. As thou hast conquered Satan and expelled him from heaven, conquer him again, and drive him far away from me at the hour of my death.

O Mary, Queen of Heaven, procure for me the assistance of Saint Michael at the hour of my death!

For the Reign of the Sacred Heart
O Mary Immaculate, great Queen of heaven and earth and our gentle advocate, we beg thee to intercede for us. Pray God to send Saint Michael and the holy angels to ward off all the obstacles contrary to the reign of the Sacred Heart in our souls, our families, our country, and in the whole world.

And thou, O holy Michael, Prince of the heavenly hosts, from our hearts we beg thee to come to our aid.

Defend us against the rage of Satan. Through the divine power bestowed on thee by God, after securing victory for the Church here below, guide our souls to our eternal home. Amen.

Saint Michael, first champion of the Kingship of Christ, pray for us!

Prayer to Saint Michael for Personal Protection
Saint Michael, the Archangel! Glorious prince, chief and champion of the heavenly hosts; guardian of the souls of men; conqueror of the rebel angels! How beautiful art thou, in thy heaven made armor. We love thee, dear prince of heaven!

We, thy happy clients, yearn to enjoy thy special protection. Obtain for us from God a share of thy sturdy courage; pray that we may have a strong and tender love for our Redeemer and, in every danger or temptation, be invincible against the enemy of our souls. O standard-bearer of our salvation! Be with us in our last moments and when our souls quit this earthly exile, carry them safely to the judgment seat of Christ, and may Our Lord and Master bid thee bear us speedily to the kingdom of eternal bliss. Teach us ever to repeat the sublime cry: "Who is like unto God?" Amen.

In Honor of All the Holy Angels

Praise the Lord, all angels of the Lord; praise him all his hosts! Almighty God, Creator of heaven and earth, I praise and thank thee, not only because thou hast created the visible world, but also because thou hast created the heavens and called the numberless spirits into being. Thou hast created them most splendidly, endowing them with power and understanding and pouring out upon them the riches of thy grace. I praise and thank thee for having showered thy graces upon the good angels, especially upon their leader, Saint Michael, and rewarded them with eternal glory after the time of their probation. Now they surround thy throne forever, singing in jubilant accord: Holy, holy, holy, Lord God of hosts! Heaven and earth are full of thy glory. Hosanna in the highest!

O Eternal God, thy holy angels serve thee with constant fidelity and ready obedience. They carry out thy commands with fervent love and sacred fervor, I thank thee, O Lord, for the example which thou hast given us through thy princes, our holy protectors. May we gladly follow the example they have given us.

Holy Archangels, Saint Michael, Saint Gabriel, and Saint Raphael, and all ye angels of the Lord, intercede for us that we may share in thy burning zeal and glowing love. Help us to become worthy messengers and true servants of God to proclaim His holy will, and to spread the peace of Christ in the Kingdom of Christ. Amen.

Prayer to Saint Michael for Paratroopers
Peter S. Griffin
101st Airborne Division
Co. A, 2/502nd PIR-DMOR
Silver Star Medal Recipient
Vietnam 1965–66
Gold Star Brother

Dear Saint Michael, protector of heaven's gate,
Guide your paratroopers, to a victorious fate.
Please keep us safe, in peace or war,
To right the wrongs, that God abhors.

Grant us speed, the flight of your wings,
The element of surprise, to deliver our sting.
Give our weapons, the fighting edge of your sword,
Equip us well, your airborne wards.

Protect our flesh, with your heavenly shield,
Your warrior heart, that we won't yield.
Grant us strength, to endure the hardships,
Fairness in dealing, with those who would harm us.

Bend your wings, to form our perimeters,
That no enemy assault, could ever wither.
Grant us courage, in attack,
Protect our flanks, and our backs.

Pray for us, on bended knee,
Lead us through hell, to victory.
To God's enemies, grant your vision to see,
That evil will fall, to those who are free.

Tell them, freedom is a gift from God,
"The Home of the Brave", His blessed sod.
"America, America, God sheds his grace on thee,"
Saint Michael, Patron Saint of Paratroopers, lead us to victory!

II. Litanies

Litany in Honor of St. Michael — I
Lord, have mercy on us.
Christ, have mercy on us.
Lord, have mercy on us.
Christ, hear us.
Christ, graciously hear us.
God the Father of Heaven, *have mercy on us.*
God the Son, Redeemer of the world, …
God the Holy Ghost,
Holy Trinity, one God,
Holy Mary, Queen of the Angels, *pray for us.*
St. Michael, the Archangel, …
Most glorious attendant of the Triune Divinity,
Standing at the right of the altar of incense,
Ambassador of Paradise,
Glorious Prince of the heavenly armies,
Leader of the angelic hosts,
The standard-bearer of God's armies,
Defender of divine glory,
First defender of the Kingship of Christ,
Strength of God,
Invincible prince and warrior,
Angel of Peace,
Guide of Christ,
Guardian of the Catholic Faith,
Champion of God's people,
Guardian Angel of the Eucharist,
Defender of the Church,

Protector of the Sovereign Pontiff,
Angel of Catholic action,
Powerful intercessor of Christians,
Bravest defender of those who hope in God,
Guardian of our souls and bodies,
Healer of the sick,
Help of those in their agony,
Consoler of the souls in purgatory,
God's messenger for the souls of the just,
Terror of the evil spirits,
Victorious in battle against evil,
Guardian and patron of the universal Church,

Lamb of God, who takest away the sins of the world, *spare us, O Lord.*

Lamb of God, who takest away the sins of the world, *graciously hear us, O Lord.*

Lamb of God, who takest away the sins of the world, *have mercy on us.*

V. Pray for us, O glorious Saint Michael.
R. *That we may be made worthy of the promises of Christ.*

Let us pray.

Relying, O Lord, upon the intercession of thy blessed Archangel Michael, we humbly beg of thee, that the Sacrament of the Eucharist which we have received may make our souls holy and pleasing to Thee. Through Christ our Lord. Amen.

Litany in Honor of St. Michael — II

Lord, have mercy on us.
Christ, have mercy on us.
Lord, have mercy on us.
Christ, hear us.
Christ, graciously hear us.
God the Father of Heaven, *have mercy on us.*
God the Son, Redeemer of the world, …
God the Holy Spirit,
Holy Trinity, one God,
Holy Mary, Queen of the Angels, *pray for us.*
Saint Michael, …
Saint Michael, filled with the wisdom of God,
Saint Michael, perfect adorer of the Incarnate Word,
Saint Michael, crowned with honor and glory,
Saint Michael, most powerful prince of the armies of the Lord,
Saint Michael, standard-bearer of the most Holy Trinity,
Saint Michael, guardian of paradise,
Saint Michael, guide and comforter of the people of Israel,
Saint Michael, splendor and fortress of the Church Militant,
Saint Michael, honor and joy of the Church Triumphant,
Saint Michael, light of angels,
Saint Michael, bulwark of orthodox believers,
Saint Michael, strength of those who fight under the standard of the cross,
Saint Michael, light and confidence of souls at the hour of death,
Saint Michael, our most sure aid,
Saint Michael, our help in all adversities,
Saint Michael, herald of the everlasting sentence,
Saint Michael, consoler of souls detained in the flames of purgatory,
Saint Michael, whom the Lord has charge to receive souls after death,
Saint Michael, our prince,
Saint Michael, our advocate,

Lamb of God, who takest away the sins of the world, *spare us O Lord.*
Lamb of God, who takest away the sins of the world, *graciously hear us O Lord.*
Lamb of God, who takest away the sins of the world, *have mercy on us.*
Christ, hear us.
Christ, graciously hear us.

V. Pray for us, O glorious Saint Michael, Prince of the Church of Jesus Christ.
R. *That we may be made worthy of his promises.*

Let us pray.

Sanctify us, we beseech thee, O Lord Jesus, with thy holy blessing, and grant us, by the intercession of Saint Michael, that wisdom which teaches us to lay up treasures in heaven by exchanging the goods of this world for those of eternity, thou who livest and reignest world without end. Amen.

III. Novena

A novena may be made at any time of the year, with any form of approved prayers. We have provided you with this one:

Saint Michael the Archangel, loyal champion of God and His Catholic people, I turn to thee with confidence and seek thy powerful intercession. For the love of God, who hast made thee so glorious in grace and power, and for the love of the Mother of Jesus, the Queen of the Angels, be pleased to hear my prayer. Thou knowest the value of my soul in the eyes of God. May no stain of evil ever disfigure its beauty. Help me to conquer the evil spirit who tempts me. I desire to imitate thy loyalty to God and Holy Mother Church and thy great love for God and men. And since thou art God's messenger for the care of His people, I entrust to thee this special request:

[Here mention your request.]

Saint Michael, since thou art, by the will of the Creator, the powerful intercessor of Christians, I have great confidence in thy prayers. I earnestly trust that if it is God's holy will, my petition will be granted.

Pray for me, Saint Michael, and also for those I love. Protect us in all dangers of body and soul. Help us in our daily needs. Through thy powerful intercession, may we live a holy life, die a happy death, and reach heaven where we may praise and love God with thee forever. Amen.

In thanksgiving to God for the graces bestowed on Saint Michael:

Our Father, Hail Mary, Glory Be.

IV. Chaplet

The Chaplet of St. Michael

O God, come to my assistance. O Lord, make haste to help me. Glory be to the Father, etc.

Say one Our Father and three Hail Marys after each of the following nine salutations in honor of the nine choirs of Angels.

1. By the intercession of Saint Michael and the celestial Choir of Seraphim may the Lord make us worthy to burn with the fire of perfect charity. Amen.

2. By the intercession of Saint Michael and the celestial Choir of Cherubim may the Lord grant us the grace to leave the ways of sin and run in the paths of Christian perfection. Amen.

3. By the intercession of Saint Michael and the celestial Choir of Thrones may the Lord infuse into our hearts a true and sincere spirit of humility. Amen.

4. By the intercession of Saint Michael and the celestial Choir of Dominations may the Lord give us grace to govern our senses and overcome any unruly passions. Amen.

5. By the intercession of Saint Michael and the celestial Choir of Powers may the Lord protect our souls against the snares and temptations of the devil. Amen.

6. By the intercession of Saint Michael and the celestial Choir of Virtues may the Lord preserve us from evil and falling into temptation. Amen.

7. By the intercession of Saint Michael and the celestial Choir of Principalities may God fill our souls with a true spirit of obedience. Amen.

8. By the intercession of Saint Michael and the celestial Choir of Archangels may the Lord give us perseverance in faith and in all good works in order that we may attain the glory of Heaven. Amen.

9. By the intercession of Saint Michael and the celestial Choir of Angels may the Lord grant us to be protected by them in this mortal life and conducted in the life to come to Heaven. Amen.

Say one Our Father in honor of each of the following leading Angels:

- Saint Michael
- Saint Gabriel
- Saint Raphael
- Your guardian angel

Concluding prayers:

O glorious prince Saint Michael, chief and commander of the heavenly hosts, guardian of souls, vanquisher of rebel spirits, servant in the house of the Divine King and our admirable conductor, you who shine with excellence and superhuman virtue deliver us from all evil, who turn to you with confidence and enable us by your gracious protection to serve God more and more faithfully every day.

V. Pray for us, O glorious Saint Michael, Prince of the Church of Jesus Christ,
R. *That we may be made worthy of His promises.*

Almighty and Everlasting God, who, by a prodigy of goodness and a merciful desire for the salvation of all men, has appointed the most glorious Archangel Saint Michael Prince of your Church, make us worthy, we ask you, to be delivered from all our enemies, that none of them may harass us at the hour of death, but that we may be conducted by him into your presence. This we ask through the merits of Jesus Christ Our Lord. Amen.

APPENDIX B
QUOTATIONS

"O great Saint Michael, take us 'neath thy shield,
Thy mighty power in our favor wield!"

— Saint John Chrysostom

"The Prince of the heavenly militia is all-powerful in purgatory, and he can assist the poor souls whom the justice and sanctity of the Almighty retain in this place of punishment."

— Saint Anselm

"It is incontestably recognized since the foundation of Christianity that the souls of the faithful departed are delivered from purgatory through the intercession of Saint Michael the Archangel."

— Saint Robert Bellarmine

"Veneration of Saint Michael is the great remedy against despising the rights of God against insubordination, skepticism and infidelity."

— Saint Francis de Sales

"Whenever any grievous temptation or vehement sorrow oppresses thee, invoke thy guardian, thy leader, cry out to him, and say, 'Lord, save us, lest we perish!"

— Saint Bernard of Clairvaux

"I have a great reverence for Saint Michael; he had no example to follow in doing the will of God, and yet he fulfilled God's will faithfully."

— Saint Faustina

"O Michael, Prince of the Morning, who didst once conquer Lucifer who wouldst make himself God, save us from our world of little gods. When the world once cracked because of a sneer in heaven, thou didst rise up and drag down from the seven heavens the pride that would look down on the Most High."

— Venerable Fulton J. Sheen

"The powers of hell will assail the dying Christian; but his angel guardian will come to console him. His patrons, and Saint Michael, who has been appointed by God to defend his faithful servants in their last combat with the devils, will come to his aid."

— Saint Alphonsus Liguori

"She beheld the glorious chief of the angelic hosts with a multitude of angels, all prepared to assist her and to combat the demons, whom she also saw under hideous forms, but so weak and powerless that they could not do her the slightest injury; and this afforded her the greatest consolation."

— *The Life and Revelations of Saint Gertrude the Great*

"In our times, when the very foundation of society is shaken in consequence of having denied the rights of God, we must revive the veneration of Saint Michael and with him raise the victorious cry: 'Who is like unto God?'"

— Cardinal Gaspar Mermillod

"All the saints and angels belong to us. We can use the intelligence of Saint Thomas Aquinas, the right arm of Saint Michael, the hearts of Joan of Arc and Catherine of Siena, and all the hidden resources which have only to be touched to be set in action."

— Paul Claudel

APPENDIX C

Hymns and Poems

Saint Michael

Frederick William Faber

Hail, bright Archangel! Prince of heaven!
Spirit divinely strong!
To whose rare merit hath been given
To head the angelic throng!

Thine the first worship was, when gloom
Through heaven's thinned ranks did move,
Thus giving unto God the bloom
Of young creation's love.

Thy zeal, with holiest awe inspired,
All other zeals outran,
With love of Mary's honor fired,
And of the Word made Man.

For God to thee, O vision glad!
The Virgin-Mother showed,
And, in His lower nature clad,
The Eternal Word of God.

Then, worshipping the splendor sent,
From out those counsels dim,
In meekest adoration bent,
Thou sangst thy voiceless hymn:

And the stars answered to thy son,
The Morning Stars of heaven;
And His first praise the angelic throng
To their Queen's Son had given.

Zealot of Jesus! from thy sword
Fling drops of gleamy fire,
To make our worship of the Word
More keenly burn and higher.

Our vile world-frozen hearts bedew
With thy celestial flame,
And burn our spirits through and through
With zeal for Jesu's Name.

O Trumpet-tongued! O Beautiful!
O Force of the Most High!
The blessed of the earth look dull
Beside thy majesty.

First servant of the Ineffable,
The first created eye,
That ever, proved and perfect, fell,
On the dread Trinity!

The strength, wherewith thy spirit dared
To love that Blissful Sight,
That mystery to the first bared
After eternal night—

That strength, O Prince! is strength to us,
Comfort and deepest joy,
That our dear God is worshipped thus
Without our base alloy.

O Michael! worship Him this night,
The Father, Word, and Dove,
Renewing with strong act the might
Of thy first marvellous love.

Glory to Him, the Eternal Dove,
Whose boundless mercy fed
His glory from thine acts of love
With condescension dread.

Praise to the Three, whose love designed
Thee champion of the Lord,
Who first conceived thee in His mind,
And made thee with His Word.

Who stooped from nothingness to raise
A life like thine so high,
Beauty and being that should praise
His love eternally!

Thy thousand thousand hosts are spread
Embattled o'er the azure sky;
But Michael bears Thy standard dread
And lifts the mighty Cross on high.
— Excerpt from "Dedication Hymn to Saint Michael"

Saint Michael (A Hymn)

Saint John Henry Newman

Thou Champion high
Of Heaven's imperial Bride,
For ever waiting on her eye,
Before her onward path, and at her side,
In war her guard secure, by night her ready guide!

To thee was given,
When those false angels rose
Against the Majesty of Heaven,
To hurl them down the steep, and on them close
The prison where they roam in hopeless unrepose.

Thee, Michael, thee,
When sight and breathing fail,
The disembodied soul shall see;
The pardon'd soul with solemn joy shall hail,
When holiest rites are spent, and tears no more avail.

And thou at last,
When time itself must die,
Shalt sound that dread and piercing blast,
To wake the dead, and rend the vaulted sky,
And summon all to meet the
Omnipotent Judge on high.

NOTES

INTRODUCTION

1. "U.S. Data Over Time," Center for Applied Research in the Apostolate, Georgetown University, https://cara.georgetown.edu/frequently-requested-church-statistics/

2. See K. E. Schmöger, *The Life and Revelations of Anne Catherine Emmerich*, vol 2 (Rockford: TAN Books, 1976), 210ff.

3. Carol Zimmerman, "Prayer to St. Michael makes resurgence in response to abuse crisis," Crux, October 4, 2018, https://cruxnow.com/church-in-the-usa/2018/10/04/prayer-to-st-michael-makes-resurgence-in-response-to-abuse-crisis/.

CHAPTER 1

1. *Catechism of the Catholic Church*, 2nd ed. (Vatican City: Vatican City Press, 1997), 328.

2. The apocryphal book from Jewish literature, *The Book of Enoch*, names seven archangels: Michael, Raphael, Gabriel, Uriel, Saraqael, Raguel, and Remiel.

CHAPTER 2

1. See Lillian Browne-Olf, *The Sword of Saint Michael: Saint Pius V, 1504–1572* (Milwaukee: The Bruce Publishing Company, 1943).

2. See chapter 4 in Ambrose, *Hexameron, Paradise, and Cain and Abel*, trans. J. Savage, *The Fathers of the Church,* vol. 42 (New York: Fathers of the Church, Inc., 1961).

3. *Latin Life of Adam and Eve*, trans. B. Custis, 21.2, https://www.marquette.edu/maqom/latinlifeadameve.html.

4. Ibid., 22.2.

5. Ibid., 28.3, 28.4, 29.1.

6. *Midrash Rabbah*, trans. H. Freedman and Maurice Simon (London: Soncino Press, 1939), 1:369.

7. Allan Menzies, ed., *The Ante-Nicene Fathers* (New York: Christian Literature Company, 1896), 9:201.

Chapter 3

1. John Charles Arnold, *The Footprints of Michael the Archangel: The Formation and Diffusion of a Saintly Cult, c. 300–c. 800* (New York: Palgrave MacMillan, 2013), 48.
2. Eusebius, *The Life of the Blessed Emperor Constantine,* in *A Select Library of Nicene and Post-Nicene Fathers of the Christian Church,* vol. I, ed. H. Wace and Philip Schaff (Oxford: Parker and Company, 1890), I.28, p. 490.
3. *The Chronicle of John Malalas* (4.12), trans. E Jeffreys et al. (Leiden: Brill, 2017), 37–38.
4. Ibid.
5. Alban Butler, *The Lives of the Primitive Fathers, Martyrs, and Other Principal Saints* (Edinburgh: J. Moir, Paterson's Court, 1799), 9:355–356.
6. Piero Marini, "Iconography and Liturgy," Vatican.va, Office of Papal Liturgical Celebrations, Published January 20, 2005, http://www.vatican.va/news_services/liturgy/2005/documents/ns_lit_doc_20050120_marini_en.html.
7. The full title of the Latin text is *Liber de apparitione de Sancti Michaelis in Monte Gargano.*
8. Ibid.
9. *Grandezze Dell' Arcangelo San Michele Nella Chiesa Trionfante, Militante, e Purgante, Parte Prima* (Rome, 1763), 248–250.
10. F. Homes Dudden, *Gregory the Great: His Place in History and Thought* (London: Longman, 1905), 1:219.
11. Ibid., 1:220.

Chapter 4

1. Harvard Divinity School, "Catholicism in France," Religious Literacy Project, accessed May 4, 2020, https://rlp.hds.harvard.edu/faq/catholicism-france
2. Gregory of Tours, *History of the Franks,* trans. Ernest Brehaut (New York: Columbia University Press, 1916), 40.
3. See Johannes Fried, *Charlemagne* (Cambridge, MA: Harvard University Press, 2016), 357ff.
4. Richard F. Johnson, *Saint Michael the Archangel in Medieval English Legend* (Woodbridge: Boydell, 2005), 43.

5. Ibid., 44.
6. See Ernst H. Kantorowicz, *Laudes Regiae: A Study in Liturgical Acclamations and Mediaeval Ruler Worship* (Berkeley: University of California Press, 1958), 15.
7. Richard North, *The Origins of Beowulf: From Vergil to Wiglaf* (Oxford: Oxford University Press, 2006), 191.
8. Helen Castor, *Joan of Arc* (New York: Harper, 2015), 43.

Chapter 5

1. Luca Amendola, "Luke Skywalker and the St. Michael Axis," January 4, 2016, https://lucaamendola.wordpress.com/2016/01/04/the-st-michael-axis/. See also Jean Richer, "Theory of Alignments," in *Sacred Geography of the Ancient Greeks*, trans. Christine Rhone (Albany: State University of New York Press, 1994), 5.
2. Edward Bourke, Alan R. Hayden, and Ann Lynch, *Skellig Michael, Co. Kerry: The Monastery and South Peak* (Government of Ireland, 2011), 21.
3. Giraldus Cambrensis, *The Topography of Ireland*, in *The Historical Works of Giraldus Cambrensis*, ed. T. Wright (London: George Bell and Sons, 1882), 134.
4. Walter Horn, Jenny White Marshall, and Grelian D. Rourke, *The Forgotten Hermitage of Skellig Michael* (Berkeley: University of California Press, 1990), 11.
5. J. R. Fletcher, *Short History of St. Michael's Mount Cornwall* (Cornwall: St. Michael's Mount, 1951), 12.
6. Officially of the High Church of England, Sunday services welcome all faiths. St. Aubyn's Estate Office email to author, August 7, 2019.
7. Geoffrey Ashe, *Avalonian Quest* (London: Methuen, 1981), 126.
8. See Nicolas Simonnet, "La Fondation du Mont-Saint-Michel d'apres la Revelatio ecclesiae sancti Michaelis," *Annales de Bretagne et des pays de l'Quest* 106, n. 4 (1999): 7–23, https://doi.org/10.3406/abpo.1999.4049
9. Richard Benke, "Welcome to Mont St. Michel, A Toy Castle Built Upon Dreams of Faith," *Los Angeles Times*, December 31, 1989, https://www.latimes.com/archives/la-xpm-1989-12-31-mn-185-story.html.

Chapter 6

1. Wentworth Webster, *Gleanings in Church History: Chiefly in Spain and France* (London: Richard Clay and Sons, 1903), 179ff.
2. The Papal Noble Guard was disbanded by Paul VI in 1970.
3. Gabriele Amorth, *An Exorcist Tells His Story* (San Francisco: Ignatius Press, 1999), 37.
4. Ibid.
5. For a complete analysis of this account, see Kevin J. Symonds, *Pope Leo XIII and the Prayer to St. Michael* (Syracuse, NY: Preserving Christian Publications, 2015).
6. Amorth, *Exorcist,* 37.
7. Henry Charles Lea, *A History of Auricular Confession and Indulgences in the Latin Church* (Philadelphia: Lea Brothers, 1896), 3:526.
8. Joseph Hilgers, "Scapular," In *The Catholic Encyclopedia* (New York: Robert Appleton Company 1912), accessed February 20, 2020 http://www.newadvent.org/cathen/13508b.htm
9. *The Roman Ritual*, trans. Philip T. Weller (Milwaukee: Bruce Publishing Company, 1964), 2:405.

Chapter 7

1. For a full account of the miracle, see Francisco de Florencia, *Narracion de la maravilloso aparición que hizo Arcángel San Miguel á Diego Lazaro de San Francisco* (Puebla: Tip. Del Colegio Pio de Artes y Oficios, 1898), 16–19.
2. Congregation for the Doctrine of the Faith, "The Message of Fatima," Vatican.va, June 26, 2000, http://www.vatican.va/roman_curia/congregations/cfaith/documents/rc_con_cfaith_doc_20000626_message-fatima_en.html
3. Ibid.
4. See Guy LoFaro, *The Sword of St. Michael: The 82nd Airborne Division in World War II* (Cambridge: Da Capo Press, 2011).
5. Daniel Wallace, "Chaplains lead St. Michael's Jump," U.S. Army, May 11, 2018, https://www.army.mil/article/205174/chaplains_lead_st_michaels_jump.

Chapter 8

1. Frederick William Faber, *The Blessed Sacrament: or, the works and ways of God* (London: Richardson and Son, 1855), 511. Eutropius was a hermit in third century Francia. Faber dedicated this work to John Henry Newman.
2. See Orthodox Church in America, "Lives of All Saints Commemorated on November 8," OCA.org, accessed May 7, 2020, https://www.oca.org/saints/all-lives/2016/11/08
3. Ibid.
4. See Orthodox Church in America, "Synaxis of the Archangel Michael and the Other Bodiless Powers — Troparion & Kontakion," OCA.org, accessed May 7, 2020 https://www.oca.org/saints/troparia/1999/11/08/103244-synaxis-of-the-archangel-michael-and-the-other-bodiless-powers
5. Ibid.
6. See "Akathist Hymn to Saint Michael the Archangel," Akathist Hymns, Reconstructed, accessed May 7, 2020, https://akathistreconstructed.wordpress.com/michael-archangel/

Chapter 9

1. *The Jewish Encyclopedia*, ed. I. Singer (New York: Funk and Wagnalls, 1904), 8:537.
2. Martin von Cochem, *The Four Last Things* (New York: Benziger Brothers, 1899), 14–15.
3. Henry Adams, *Mont-Saint-Michel and Chartres* (New York: Penguin Books, 1986), 7.
4. Paul Kengor, "John Paul II's Warning on 'Final Confrontation' With the 'Anti-Church,'" *National Catholic Register*, October 5, 2018, http://www.ncregister.com/daily-news/john-paul-iis-warning-on-final-confrontation-with-the-anti-church.

Chapter 10

1. von Cochem, 89.
2. Ibid., 109–10.

About the Author

James Day is a writer, filmmaker, and television production manager for EWTN. Raised in an Irish-American home in a largely Catholic neighborhood of Independence, Ohio, outside Cleveland, Day earned a BA in Latin with minors in English and History and a concentration in Catholic Studies at John Carroll University. Among his professors were Dr. Thomas R. Nevin, Dr. Phil Metres, and Dr. Francesco Cesareo, current president of Assumption College and chair of the USCCB's National Review Board for the Protection of Children and Young People. Day followed with a Masters of Fine Arts in Film Production at Loyola Marymount University. He has produced a number of festival-screened short films, one of which, *The Passion of Veronica*, a dystopian thriller set in the near future where Catholicism is outlawed, was nominated for Best Short Film at the Vatican's Mirabile Dictu Film Festival in 2014. He currently manages EWTN's Orange County television studio, which produces original content in Spanish and English, including *Father Spitzer's Universe*. Day is the author of two previous books, one on Pope Emeritus Benedict XVI, *Father Benedict* (2016, Sophia Institute Press), and *A Place for Christ Forever: Becoming Christ Cathedral* (2019), with a foreword by Cardinal Robert Sarah. He has a book in development on Catholicism and Hollywood's Golden Age and is currently researching the history of the Shroud of Turin.